Of Mice and Men

John Steinbeck

Guide written and developed by
John Mahoney and Stewart Martin

Charles Letts & Co Ltd
London, Edinburgh & New York

First published 1987
by Charles Letts & Co Ltd
Diary House, Borough Road, London SE1 1DW

Illustrations: Peter McClure

Stewart Martin is an Honours graduate of Lancaster University, where he read English
and Sociology. He has worked both in the UK and abroad as a writer, a teacher, and an
educational consultant. He is married with three children, and is currently deputy
headmaster at Ossett School in West Yorkshire.

John Mahoney has taught English for twenty years. He has been head of English
department in three schools and has wide experience of preparing students at all levels
for most examination boards. He has worked both in the UK and North America
producing educational books and computer software on English language and literature.
He is married with three children and lives in Worcestershire.

British Library Cataloguing in Publication Data
  Mahoney, John
  Of mice and men: John Steinbeck: guide.
  (Guides to literature)
  I. Steinbeck, John 1902–1968. Of mice
  and men
  I. Title   II. Martin, Stewart
  III. Steinbeck, John, 1902–1968. Of mice
  and men   IV. Series
  813'.52   PS3537.T323403

ISBN 0 85097 772 X

Printed and bound in Great Britain by
Charles Letts (Scotland) Ltd

Contents

To the student

This study companion to your English literature text acts as a guide to the novel or play being studied. It suggests ways in which you can explore content and context, and focuses your attention on those matters which will lead to an understanding, appreciative and sensitive response to the work of literature being studied.

Whilst covering all those aspects dealt with in the traditional-style study aid, more importantly, it is a flexible companion to study, enabling you to organize the patterns of study and priorities which reflect your particular needs at any given moment.

Whilst in many places descriptive, it is never prescriptive, always encouraging a sensitive personal response to a work of literature, rather than the shallow repetition of others' opinions. Such objectives have always been those of the good teacher, and have always assisted the student to gain high grades in 16+ examinations in English literature. These same factors are also relevant to students who are doing coursework in English literature for the purposes of continual assessment.

The major part of this guide is the 'Commentary' where you will find a detailed commentary and analysis of all the important things you should know and study for your examination. There is also a section giving practical help on how to study a set text, write the type of essay that will gain high marks, prepare coursework and a guide to sitting examinations.

Used sensibly, this guide will be invaluable in your studies and help ensure your success in the course.

John Steinbeck

John Steinbeck was born in 1902 at Salinas in California, the son of a part-German father and an Irish mother. He graduated from Salinas High School in 1919 and then went on to a fairly desultory university career at Stanford, leaving in 1925 without earning a degree. He began university by studying English, but then studied a variety of courses according to his interests and took much time off.

In the years that followed he had a great many casual jobs from newspaper work to that of the intinerant ranch-hand and, although he had some local success as a writer, it was not until the publication of *Of Mice and Men* in January/February 1937, a book described as 'prose-drama', that he won international recognition. He had probably been writing *Of Mice and Men* since early 1935, when he had mentioned that he was writing a play. By the date of the publication of the novelette Steinbeck had already established himself as a writer interested in contemporary issues, and so his readers would probably not have been surprised that this book had as its background agricultural labour in California. What most of his readers might have expected however, was something about strikes, Communist agitators and the like. But the workers in *Of Mice and Men* are non-political – they accept their lot in life and never question the society in which they live. The book was an immediate and widespread success.

Originally called 'Something that Happened', the book was retitled from a line in a poem by Robert Burns:

> 'The best laid schemes o' mice an' men
>   Gang aft a-gley   [astray]
> An' lea'e us nought but grief an' pain
>   For promised joy!'

Burns' poem was entitled 'To a Mouse, on Turning Her Up in Her Nest, with the Plow, November, 1785' but Steinbeck's original title might be just as revealing. Does the title 'Something that Happened' suggest that the events in the book are of no real consequence, or are commonplace? Do you think that *Of Mice and Men* is predominantly a hopeful or a hopeless story? Consider whether you feel that the ending of the story was inevitable or whether you feel that it might have been possible for George and Lennie to actually have ended up owning their own farm. If you feel that the book is depressing in its view of the itinerants' lives and prospects, consider how far its outcome seems to you to be predestined. Does the book offer any redeeming or hopeful view of the itinerants' relationships with each other? Does it offer any future for them – any possibility of happiness?

The story is conceived as a narrative in three acts, with each of the six sections of the book equivalent to a scene. Each section, or scene, is introduced by a detailed descriptive setting followed by economically expressed dialogue. The publication of the book in novel form was followed in the same year by a stage play, which won an award for the best New York play of 1937.

The main characters in the story, Lennie and George, are itinerant farm workers, and Steinbeck, in the novel, is highlighting a social problem of immense proportions, which he had experienced at firsthand. Climatic changes in the west of America between 1880 and 1930 resulted in the death through drought of large tracts of fertile land which had supported the early homesteaders. These were settlers who had established the sort of small farms that represent the 'promised joy' of the workers in the story. They were driven from the land by the harsh changes of climate that eventually resulted in the 'Great American Dust Bowl', and they desperately searched for work in the remaining fertile regions. These itinerant American workers, compounded in number by the unemployed as a result of the Thirties' slump, replaced the traditional immigrant Mexican labour. Since they were available in great numbers they were exploited by farm owners who employed them on low rates of pay and in appalling conditions. These men were only in demand for short periods at a time and they had to save enough from seasonal work, such as harvesting of crops and fruits, to support them through the rest of the year. Because of their insular and solitary lifestyle, and their extreme mobility, little could be done to organize their protection through trade union membership. This was of great concern to Steinbeck, who dealt with the problem in this novel, in *In Dubious Battle,* and also in his most successful book *The Grapes of Wrath,* which won the Pulitzer Prize in 1940.

John Steinbeck died in 1969, his subsequent books not enjoying the popularity of his earlier work.

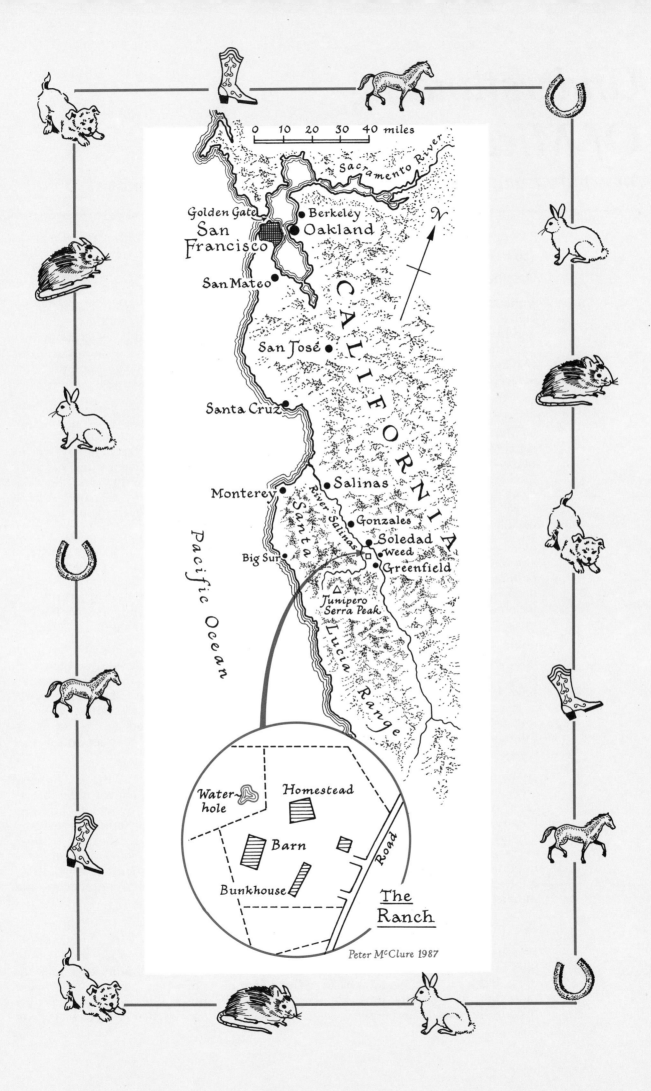

0 10 20 30 40 miles

Sacramento River

Golden Gate
San Francisco
Berkeley
Oakland

San Mateo

CALIFORNIA

San José

Santa Cruz

Salinas

Monterey

Santa

River Salinas

Gonzales

Soledad
weed
Greenfield

Big Sur

Junipero
Serra Peak

Santa Lucia Range

Pacific Ocean

Water-hole
Homestead

Barn

Bunkhouse

Road

The Ranch

Peter McClure 1987

Understanding
Of Mice and Men

An exploration of the major topics and themes in the novel

Summaries of themes

Aspects of style

Various aspects of Steinbeck's style are clearly evident in *Of Mice and Men*. We see his skill in revealing important aspects of the development of the story a little at a time. A good example of this is the incident with the girl in Weed, where it takes us about forty pages to get a complete picture of what happened. Steinbeck is economical in his play/novel structure: many allusions have a significance later in the plot and therefore act as portents, and the background of the novel is carefully described.

The book's format of play/novel makes extraneous description rare and there is little comedy in the novel, although some aspects of Lennie's behaviour are comic. Instead, *Of Mice and Men* is a kind of tragedy. The word 'tragedy' is used in the Greek dramatic sense, thus the central character, Lennie, dies as the result of the 'fatal flaw' in his personality. In this case it is a striving for affection, manifested by his need for 'petting'. The book is also a tragedy in the sense that the lives and fates of the main characters are not rooted in an ordered society – they live in a world where normal social order and normal human relationships have been destroyed. Their lives are usually directionless and chaotic as a result.

Steinbeck also uses sounds and colours deliberately, as when Curley's wife is associated with red; this is especially pointed because Lennie has been likened to a bull, but red has other symbolic images (blood, fire or passion for example). Sound is used with great skill, as in a film, to shape the atmosphere surrounding events – we feel enclosed in silence at some points and at others overwhelmed by a cacophony of noise (the scene after the murder of Curley's wife is a good example of the former).

Steinbeck uses other theatrical devices to make *Of Mice and Men* function at times like a book and at times like a play – a fluidity of style which suits a play/novel and Steinbeck carefully exploits the best of both types of medium to suit the occasion. Some critics have detected semi-religious echoes in the work. Lennie, in his 'raw' state of innocence is in sight of 'paradise', but his entanglement with Curley's wife, motivated by an unconscious desire for affection, damns him and he is sacrificed because of man's inhumanity. Because of this 'sin', the 'paradise', symbolized by the rabbits and several times described by George, is lost to him.

As with the rest of the themes discussed here, good examples of all these aspects of style are pointed out and discussed in the commentary whenever they occur. However, always use your own sensitivity and understanding when reading any literary work. No list of themes, however complete, can ever totally define or 'explain' any good piece of literature. Even the themes mentioned here are not dealt with on every single occasion when they can be seen in action – only some of their most important and interesting manifestations are drawn to your attention. This study guide is designed to get you started on your own road to enjoyment and understanding – it is not a completed highway.

Authority

Various forms of authority are present in the novel – from the God-like authority of Slim to the ineffectual, bullying authority of Curley. The boss's authority is, like his dress, black and severe, and is based on exploitation. George's authority over Lennie is more difficult to classify; it has elements of the same authority which Candy has over his dog, but sometimes Lennie is able to reverse its action, as when he threatens to run away.

Several characters use violence or financial power as the basis of their authority, whilst others seem to have personal authority because they avoid any form of exploitation. Generally, those who use the first kind of base for their authority are unable to understand the values and drives of characters who do not – Carlson and Curley cannot fathom the distress of Slim and George at the end of the novel, for example.

Dreams

Many of the characters have dreams – in the sense that they have hopes or ambitions. Interestingly these dreams are often kept secret to begin with: we know that George and Lennie have a dream which they hide from others. (Remember how George is displeased when he discovers that Lennie and Candy have told Crooks about it.) In contrast, Curley's wife seems almost desperate to tell Lennie about her dreams when they are in the barn. It is one of the great ironies of the book that she should decide to confide in someone who appears to have no interest in, or capability of, understanding.

The 'dream farm' represents ambition and escape from the itinerants' tradition of loneliness and poverty. The 'dream' element also encompasses the ambition of Curley's wife to evade reality. Many of the workers have dreams and sometimes they share the same dream. Generally speaking there is usually a choice of two types of dream open to them – the dream which includes companionship, openness and love (like the 'dream farm' idea) and the dream of a solitary state which excludes all human contact like George's vision at the end of the book when he sees his future as an unending cycle of aimless drifting: '. . . I'll take my fifty bucks an' I'll stay all night in some lousy cat-house. Or I'll set in some pool-room till ever'body goes home.' Both states are equally 'safe' for characters (although not equally satisfying) if they can remain wholly within one or the other. Danger threatens whenever a character moves to try to reach a different dream.

Loneliness

Many of the characters, by virtue of their itinerant existence, are lonely, and their loneliness motivates them to seek alternative ways of life. This is one of the reasons why they are drifters – they are continually searching, often without knowing what they are really looking for. All of these characters are also lonely because of something within themselves – something which almost seems to make their loneliness inevitable. Different characters seek solace in different things – for Candy it is his dog, for George and Lennie it is each other, and for characters like Crooks it is his pride and such things as his unerring skill at pitching horseshoes.

The natural world

The world of nature, including the landscape and animals, plays a large part in the events of the novel. Lennie is often described as a 'bear' and natural environments and attendant animals surround him throughout. Lennie himself is 'natural', that is he has the simplicity and innocence of all animals. The peacefulness of nature is depicted several times throughout the novel, and provides a pastoral calm which is shown as being destroyed only by man. The itinerants' life is unnatural in that theirs is a rootless existence outside of any 'proper' society. They are like men adrift in the wilderness.

The behaviour of humans towards animals finds a parallel in the way humans behave towards their fellow beings as, for example, when the death of Candy's dog provides a parallel to Lennie's death. Candy's dog is at the end of its useful life and the humane killing is justified by some of the men because of this; if judged in the same kind of way the killing of Lennie is also the only 'humane' choice.

The needs of animals are shown as not always being appropriate when they surface in the unnatural world of man. For example, Slim's gift of a puppy helps in the escalation of Lennie's 'petting' activities, which culminate in the accidental killing of Curley's wife.

Steinbeck also uses animals in their natural world to reinforce the thematic structure of the book, as when the snake that appears at the beginning of the novel dies at the end. The world of nature is seen as filled with powerful spiritual forces – as when, at the beginning of the book, the large carp 'sank mysteriously into the dark water again.'

Violence

The world of the men in the book is filled with unnecessary and gratuitous violence. The boss is a good example of this in the way he treats the men and permits fighting. Curley is another good example with his almost completely irrational belligerence – as George remarks at their first meeting: 'Say, what the hell's he got on his shoulder?' Carlson is another example of a character who seems to thrive on violence, both in argument and in goading others, and in the evident pleasure with which he demonstrates the effectiveness of his Luger on Candy's dog. The gun's availability, and Carlson's unthinking but detailed explanation of his killing technique, give to George the means of dispatching Lennie. As you read the book try to see if you can identify exactly why each violent character behaves in the way he does.

Analysis chart

	Friday evening			Saturday															Sunday					
Day	Friday evening			Saturday															Sunday					
Section	1			2						3						4			5				6	
Comment numbers (from–to)	1–16	17–19	20–31	32–35	36–41	42–52	53–58	59–64	65–66	67–76	77–79	80–86	87–100	101–106	107–123	124–143	144–157	158–176	177–180	181–191	192–195	196–213	214–217	218–222
Location	The pool			The bunkhouse												The harness room			The great barn				The pool	
Important events	George and Lennie arrive at the pool	The dead mouse is handed over	First mention of the dream ranch	George and Lennie arrive at the bunkhouse	The boss interviews them	Curley arrives	Curley's wife appears	Slim and Carlson arrive	The possibility of a puppy!	Slim is told about Lennie and events in Weed	Lennie brings his puppy to bed	Carlson shoots Candy's dog	Curley goes to the barn looking for Slim	Candy overhears about the dream ranch	Curley fights Lennie – to his cost	Lennie visits Crooks – who taunts him	Candy arrives. They share the dream	Curley's wife appears. She shatters the dream	Lennie has 'petted' his puppy to death	Curley's wife arrives. She and Lennie talk	Lennie 'pets' Curley's wife to death. He runs away	A posse sets out after Lennie	Lennie arrives at the pool. He sees visions	George shoots Lennie

Themes

Theme	1–16	17–19	20–31	32–35	36–41	42–52	53–58	59–64	65–66	67–76	77–79	80–86	87–100	101–106	107–123	124–143	144–157	158–176	177–180	181–191	192–195	196–213	214–217	218–222
Aspects of style	●	●	●	●	●	●	●	●		●	●	●	●	●	●	●	●	●	●	●	●	●	●	●
Authority								●					●	●	●		●	●				●		●
Dreams	●		●										●	●	●		●			●	●	●	●	●
Loneliness								●		●	●		●	●		●	●		●	●	●	●		
The natural world	●	●	●	●			●	●	●	●	●		●	●	●	●	●	●	●	●	●	●	●	
Violence				●	●	●	●	●	●	●	●		●	●	●	●		●		●		●		●

Characters

Character	1–16	17–19	20–31	32–35	36–41	42–52	53–58	59–64	65–66	67–76	77–79	80–86	87–100	101–106	107–123	124–143	144–157	158–176	177–180	181–191	192–195	196–213	214–217	218–222
Candy				●	●	●							●	●	●	●	●	●				●		
Carlson								●				●	●	●	●		●					●		●
Crooks																●	●	●						
Curley						●	●	●		●				●		●		●		●	●	●		
Curley's wife							●	●		●		●			●			●	●	●	●	●		
George	●		●		●	●	●	●		●			●	●	●	●	●	●	●	●		●	●	●
Lennie	●	●	●		●	●	●	●		●	●	●	●	●	●	●	●	●	●	●	●	●	●	●
Slim							●			●	●	●	●	●	●	●		●					●	●
The boss				●	●																			
Whit												●	●											

(Handwritten annotation at lower left: "+ prejudice + relationships"; star/cross marks beside the theme and character labels.)

Finding your way around the commentary

Each page of the commentary gives the following information:

1 A quotation from the start of each paragraph on which a comment is made, or act/scene or line numbers plus a quotation, so that you can easily locate the right place in your text.

2 A series of comments, explaining, interpreting, and drawing your attention to important incidents, characters and aspects of the text.

3 For each comment, headings to indicate the important characters, themes, and ideas dealt with in the comment.

4 For each heading, a note of the comment numbers in this guide where the previous or next comment dealing with that heading occurred.

Thus you can use this commentary section in a number of ways.

1 Turn to that part of the commentary dealing with the chapter/act (or in this novel, section) you are perhaps revising for a class discussion or essay. Read through the comments in sequence, referring all the time to the text, which you should have open before you. The comments will direct your attention to all the important things of which you should take note.

2 Take a single character or topic from the list opposite. Note the comment number next to it. Turn to that comment in this guide, where you will find the first of a number of comments on your chosen topic. Study it, and the appropriate part of your text to which it will direct you. Note the comment number in this guide where the next comment for your topic occurs and turn to it when you are ready. Thus, you can follow one topic right through your text. If you have an essay to write on a particular character or theme just follow the path through this guide and you will soon find everything you need to know!

3 A number of relevant relationships between characters and topics are listed on the opposite page. To follow these relationships throughout your text, turn to the comment indicated. As the previous and next comment are printed at the side of each page in the commentary, it is a simple matter to flick through the pages to find the previous or next occurrence of the relationship in which you are interested.

For example, you want to examine in depth the theme of 'loneliness' in the novel. Turning to the single topic list, you will find that this theme first occurs in comment 63. On turning to comment 63 you will discover a zero (0) in the place of the previous reference (because this is the first time that it has occurred) and the number 73 for the next reference. You now turn to comment 73 and find that the previous comment number is 63 (from where you have just been looking) and that the next reference is to comment 79, and so on throughout the text.

You also wish to trace the thematic relationship between 'loneliness' and 'dreams' throughout the novel. From the relationships list, you are directed to comment 104. This is the first time that both 'loneliness' and 'dreams' are discussed together and you will now discover that two different comment numbers are given for the subject under examination – numbers 136 and 112. This is because each theme is traced separately as well as together and you will have to continue tracing them separately until you finally come to comment 146 – the next occasion on which both 'loneliness' and 'dreams' are discussed.

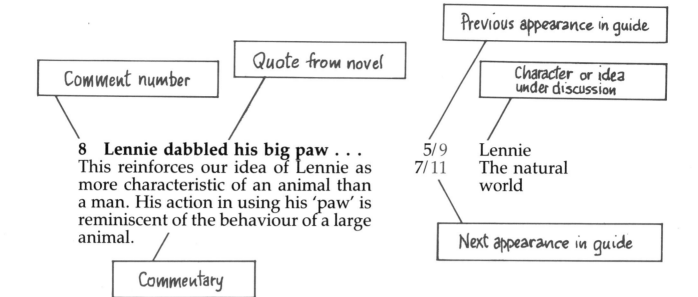

Comment number

Quote from novel

Previous appearance in guide

Character or idea under discussion

8 Lennie dabbled his big paw . . .
This reinforces our idea of Lennie as more characteristic of an animal than a man. His action in using his 'paw' is reminiscent of the behaviour of a large animal.

Commentary

5/9   Lennie
7/11   The natural world

Next appearance in guide

Single topics:

	Comment no:		Comment no:
Aspects of style	1	Candy	34
Authority	60	Carlson	62
Dreams	15	Crooks	124
Loneliness	63	Curley	41
The natural world	1	Curley's wife	49
Violence	35	George	2
		Lennie	2
		Slim	59
		The boss	33
		Whit	84

Because *Of Mice and Men* has elements of allegory in it, many of the characters and themes are closely bound up with one another. There is considerable 'overlap' as far as relationships are concerned and you should not assume that because a particular relationship is not listed below it is not present in the novel, or is not important.

The following list of relationships is not exhaustive, nor is it meant to be. For example, almost any character can be found to have an interesting relationship with any theme, or any other character. 'Aspects of style' can similarly be found in interesting association with most characters and themes. It has not been identified where these can first be found as they are easily located within the commentary. What have been identified below are, instead, some interesting relationships which exist between some of the themes and images. But remember, in the final analysis it is the understanding and interpretation which *you* draw from your reading which is most important. This list simply provides a useful jumping-off point for your own ideas.

Relationships:

			Comment no:
The natural world	and	Authority	83
	and	Dreams	101
	and	Loneliness	79
Loneliness	and	Authority	170
	and	Dreams	104
Violence	and	Authority	60
	and	Loneliness	73
	and	The natural world	58

Section 1

*Having come from the town of Weed,
George and Lennie spend the night at the pool,
prior to travelling on to the ranch.*

Commentary

Characters and ideas
previous/next comment

1 Evening of a hot day . . .

The introductory idea of nature disturbed by man becomes more and more obvious in this section as, at the 'sound of footsteps' the natural inhabitants flee. This movement from harmony to discord is to appear in most of the detailed settings that Steinbeck creates. Notice the way in which nature is often described in the book. Steinbeck concentrates our attention on atmosphere. Of what biblical place does the book's opening description remind you? (Hint: look at Genesis.) Compare the two descriptions of the pool here at the beginning of the book and also at the end. Why is the atmosphere different in the two scenes? Look at how the effect is achieved.

0/6   Aspects of style

0/4   The natural world

2 Evening of a hot day . . .   — casual

This presents us with the familiar image of itinerant workers: drifters who move from ranch to ranch, skilled in various aspects of farm work, in the traditional dress of cowboys, from whom they descend. Lennie follows George, and the description of the appearance of both of them contributes to our understanding of their characters. George, 'every part of him defined', gives the immediate impression of intelligence and we are reminded of some sort of quick-witted animal by his 'restless' ways. He leads the pair; and from this and his general behaviour we can see that he is clearly the one who is in charge.

0/3   George

0/4   Lennie

3 The first man stopped short . . .

This furthers our understanding of George. Both of the men have endured some physical hardship. George takes stock of the situation and relieves his discomfort in traditional cowboy style. He is a cautious type of person.

2/5   George

4 The first man stopped short . . .

There is a strong animal flavour in the portrayal of Lennie, who is described as a 'bear'. The animal context is important, because it establishes at once the essential element in Lennie's character – the welding of his brute strength to his animal-like innocence. The bear is a particularly appropriate image, because the bear shares not only Lennie's harmless looks (as in a teddy-bear) but also his tendency to hold on to things in his 'bear-hug'. In the case of both creatures, few survive such gestures of affection! Notice how Steinbeck's description creates a vivid image of Lennie's movements.

2/5   Lennie

1/5   The natural world

5 'Lennie!' he said sharply.

This reinforces the suggestion that Lennie is a man with a markedly animal temperament. He is devoid of caution and drinks copiously despite the fact that the pool is 'green'. Notice how Steinbeck on this occasion compares Lennie with a horse. These images are emphasizing Lennie's animal-like innocence. Like an animal Lennie fulfils his immediate desires – in this case for water – and seems unable to see the possible consequences even though, as George observes, it was only the previous night that he was sick. This attitude is a forewarning of future events. One of Lennie's most dangerous failings is his inability to learn from past experience. George's admonishment establishes his role as Lennie's mentor (or keeper), and he has

3/7   George

4/8   Lennie

4/7   The natural world

obviously taken on the responsibility of protecting Lennie from himself. In this incident George is ill at ease and apprehensive. Why?

The description of Lennie and George concentrates on the way their characters seem to fit together very well – they 'suit' each other because of their complementary natures. Both men are dressed in the same way, but in temperament Lennie is slow where George is quick; he is clumsy whilst George is precise; he is unconsciously confident where George is apprehensive and nervous. Lennie suffers as a consequence of his impetuous and reckless behaviour.

6 Lennie dipped his whole head . . .
Some aspects of Lennie's behaviour contribute to the humour of the novel. His action here in dipping 'his whole head under, hat and all' is visually comic.

1/9	Aspects of style

7 George unslung his bundle . . .
George shows intelligence and this example demonstrates his knowledge of possible threats to them from the environment. He knows that standing water is dangerous, and that 'You never oughta drink water when it ain't running'.

5/9	George
5/8	The natural world

8 Lennie dabbled his big paw . . .
This reinforces our idea of Lennie as more characteristic of an animal than a man. His action in using his 'paw' is reminiscent of the behaviour of a large animal.

5/9	Lennie
7/11	The natural world

9 George knelt beside the pool . . .
This strengthens our understanding of the relationship between Lennie and George. Not only is George Lennie's mentor, but clearly Lennie 'looks up' to him as a model of correct behaviour. Lennie is also trying to please George with his actions.

6/10	Aspects of style
7/12	George
8/10	Lennie

This exposition, (or the filling in of events before the story opens) puts the relationship between Lennie and George into a slightly wider context. If they are treated in this disdainful and casual way by a bus driver, then their status must be quite low, because they have been badly treated by someone holding a fairly menial position. Is it possible, then, that this is the first indication of why George actually needs Lennie to care for? Does George actually need Lennie more than Lennie needs George? If so, would this imbue Lennie with some sort of human dignity as opposed to his natural, animal-like state of innocence? Look at the George-Lennie relationship as you read the text and this guide; try to see why they stay together and exactly what each puts into and gets out of their relationship.

10 'Where we goin', George?'
Lennie is not able to remember things easily. Such a device allows Steinbeck an opportunity to provide us with some background material and in this instance, having now established the characters and relationship of George and Lennie, he gently moves the narrative forward.

9/14	Aspects of style
9/11	Lennie

11 'The hell with the rabbits.'
This is the first slight hint of trouble to come. It mentions what has caused them to be on the run from their last employment. We have associated Lennie with the uncomplicated innocence of an animal. This is the first suggestion that this animal-like behaviour must include an unconscious, instinctive search for a mate and for companionship.

10/12   Lennie
8/12   The natural world

12 'Oh, sure, George. I remember that now.'
This episode follows Lennie's 'delighted smile' when he remembered 'some girls'. This physical 'petting' of small animals fulfils Lennie's need for some sort of physical contact. It is the merest hint at one aspect of his personality – one that is resolved by the tragic end of the novel. He is unable to control his need to display this 'warmth' and is also unable to discriminate between living and dead creatures.

9/13   George
11/13   Lennie
11/17   The natural world

As the novel unfolds, notice how Lennie's fatal petting progresses through a dead mouse to little girls, to hoped-for rabbits, to a puppy, and finally to Curley's wife. George shouts 'Give it here' at Lennie, demonstrating the need at times for forceful authority in controlling him. This extends our notion of George's role from companion to include a parental figure, and establishes a relationship which includes reprimands for Lennie's child-like behaviour. Do you think it is also a master and animal relationship?

George and Lennie can be seen as the two halves of one complete individual – one being the intelligence and one the body. In a psychological sense we can see that George is the rational one who is in control of the 'whole individual' and Lennie is the one full of basic animal desires or 'earth longings' as Steinbeck calls them.

13 'Aw, leave me have it, George.'
There is great variety in the mood of the relationship between Lennie and George. George moves very quickly from stern firmness and absolute demands to endeavouring to instil good behaviour by kinder means. This accentuates the child-like response that Lennie produces. George's advice sometimes leads to trouble – as it does in this instance.

12/15   George
12/14   Lennie

14 'Sure, George. Sure I got it.'
First, Steinbeck revealed some past trouble with 'girls', now we see that the pair have recently been hounded out of their last employment. Lennie has done 'bad things' which caused the need for them to escape. The fact that Lennie 'giggled' at the thought makes the incident sound less serious than it was – but in fact he had a close shave with death. This is excellent narrative technique: Steinbeck is slowly revealing to us the enormity of the event and its consequences for Lennie and George. This way of writing engages the readers by drawing them into the story, whetting their appetite and keeping them continually interested.

10/17   Aspects of style
13/15   Lennie

15 George lay back on the sand . . .
This is the first example of dreams of better things in the future. Such dreams become increasingly important as the novel progresses. Why does George remain with Lennie? The answer to this question is buried in the complex nature of the relationship between them. The question also hints at the hidden implications of including the companionship of a girl as one of George's aspirations.

0/27   Dreams
13/16   George
14/16   Lennie

	Characters and ideas previous/*next* comment

16 For a moment Lennie lay quiet . . .
George appreciates the stillness and the harmony of the pastoral scene. This moment of calm interrupts the interplay of the two characters before the parental relationship is reintroduced by Lennie's petulant demand for 'ketchup' with his beans. This skilful touch reveals a nice piece of observation on Steinbeck's part. As students will know, Lennie's demand is still one that is immensely popular!

15/22   George
15/18   Lennie

17 The day was going fast now.
This pastoral interlude links up with the opening of the novel and re-establishes a sense of harmony. It also introduces a gentler tone. Notice how the water-snake becomes a victim at the end of the novel, producing discord where harmony once prevailed. The description appeals to our senses of hearing and sight and we are encouraged to see the natural world as an innocent child might.

14/19   Aspects of style
12/18   The natural world

18 Lennie lumbered to his feet . . .
This episode stresses the importance Lennie attributes to the need for something to pet. He is prepared to hunt around for the carcass and is desperately evasive when asked to hand over the mouse.

16/19   Lennie
17/19   The natural world

19 'What mouse, George? I ain't got no mouse.'
This incident tells us more about Lennie's need for some way of expressing affection. Steinbeck again uses animal imagery to describe Lennie as 'like a terrier'. A characteristic which Lennie and a terrier both share is their tendency to hold on to things. The episode prepares us for things to come: Lennie is reluctant to let go of the mouse; he has 'broken' it by petting it; he has killed other small creatures (or 'pinched their heads a little' as Lennie puts it); he wants something that is living. These are inclinations, here revealed in miniature, that are going to have devastating consequences in the future.

17/21   Aspects of style
18/20   Lennie
17/21   The natural world

20 The flame of the sunset lifted . . .
The flow of the narrative is interrupted by a pastoral description that restores peace and harmony. However, notice that there is a powerful sense of hidden things emerging – as in the way in which the 'big carp' rises, then sinks 'mysteriously' leaving 'widening rings' similar to those created by Lennie's 'paw' earlier. Does this mirror the increasing repercussions of Lennie's actions during the course of the novel? Certainly the suggestion that Lennie has mysterious or subconscious depths to his behaviour would fit this idea.

19/21   Lennie
19/21   The natural world

21 'Well, we ain't got any,' George exploded.
Steinbeck has been building up to this revelation. Having generated a sense of curiosity about events which happened before the novel opens, he now illustrates the serious nature of Lennie's actions and the relationship between petting mice and the girls that delighted him. He is unaware of the basic drives and desires that prompt his actions and his 'innocent' gestures have been misinterpreted by others, who have jumped to what they thought were fair conclusions. Think about Lennie for a moment – does his state of mind resemble that of a mentally retarded person, and that of someone wholly without malice or evil? Does Lennie's innocence and purity echo that of the surrounding world of nature? If you think it does, can you identify the

19/25   Aspects of style
20/22   Lennie
20/23   The natural world

method Steinbeck has used to suggest this? (Hint: look at the imagery with which Lennie is usually associated.)

The place in which they find themselves is a 'few miles south of Soledad'—which is an actual place in California. Soledad is a Spanish name meaning both loneliness and a lonely place. Notice how George describes himself and Lennie as the sort of people who 'are the loneliest guys in the world.' Although the boss thinks that George exploits Lennie, notice how all the ranch-hands eventually come to see that the reason for their relationship is mutual loneliness.

22 'Well, we ain't got any,' George exploded.

This is a reintroduction of one of George's preoccupations. The alternative life-style that he mentions is fairly limited: drink, food, hired women and gambling. It is the life-style which the other workers in the story also find so unsatisfying. George, by teaming up with Lennie, enjoys companionship and a sense of responsibility—rewards greater than the empty experience of the common itinerant worker about whom he keeps talking. Perhaps Lennie's terror at the prospect of being abandoned is the motive for George's speculation. The question of why he doesn't strike off on his own is one you should think about. What would you have done if you had been George?

16/23   George
21/23   Lennie

23 It was quite dark now . . .

That George 'looked ashamedly' indicates that he is sorry for the pain he has caused Lennie. Notice how the animal imagery constantly accompanies Lennie—here in his 'slowly and cautiously' crawling round the fire, with the wariness of an animal. He is upset by George's rejection of him and tries to make amends in a child-like way.

22/24   George
22/24   Lennie
21/24   The natural
        world

24 Lennie still knelt.

Lennie's suggestion is in keeping with the way in which Steinbeck has used animal comparisons throughout. The solution Lennie offers is characteristic of an animal—living in a cave and lying in the sun—and is particularly appropriate for a bear, which has dominated Steinbeck's description of Lennie so far. This points to the strange kind of animal intellect which Lennie displays—an intelligence which is based on intuition. Of course Lennie's suggestion is not welcomed by George, not only because Lennie would not survive (or would he?), but because George, despite his constant explosions of temperament, needs Lennie. Consider again why George needs Lennie. We might guess fairly easily what Lennie gets out of their relationship, but George also profits from his relationship with Lennie in several ways. He gets physical protection, he gets a feeling of doing something good and noble in looking after him, and he gets a boost to his own self-esteem, because Lennie makes him feel superior. Notice that he also gets an excuse for his own failure to make much of himself, and he later admits as much to Slim when he confesses that 'I ain't so bright neither.'

23/25   George
23/25   Lennie
23/25   The natural
        world

Notice how, after Lennie has killed Curley's wife, George has little interest in their 'dream farm'. Although George is not Lennie's relative, he tells the boss that he is his 'cousin'. George acts as Lennie's protector. How do you think the other characters in *Of Mice and Men* regard one another? Do they also protect and care for each other?

25 'No–look! I was jus' foolin', Lennie.'
Lennie has gained the initiative with his threat to move into a cave and George seems to sense a danger to himself and a threat to the security of their companionship. By way of compensation George unwittingly offers Lennie the instrument of his downfall. Later, it is because of the puppy that Lennie spends so much time in the barn. It is one of the characteristics of fate that it takes even the best intentions of people and uses them to adverse effect. With hindsight, there seems to be an awful inevitability in the way that these separate strands are carefully and unerringly woven together. In fact it is a tribute to Steinbeck's skill as a writer that this feeling pervades the climax of the story.

21/26	Aspects of style
24/26	George
24/26	Lennie
24/30	The natural world

26 Lennie avoided the bait.
George's comment to Lennie that 'Somebody'd shoot you for a coyote' is an important contribution to the working out of the plot. It is ironic in that *he* is the one to shoot Lennie in the way in which Candy's old dog is shot by Carlson. In *Of Mice and Men* Steinbeck weaves his ideas very closely indeed, and sometimes remarks which seem at the time to be entirely casual later turn out to carry the weight of the whole narrative. The portentous expressions here contribute to a gathering sense of doom. It is ironic that George, in attempting to keep Lennie from harm, actually causes it and is the instrument of his subsequent downfall.

25/30	Aspects of style
25/27	George
25/27	Lennie

27 Lennnie pleaded: . . .
Lennie enjoys this promise of a better life, as a child enjoys a familiar fairy story or folk-tale. But this myth that George has put together represents far more than that. The 'paradise', or 'heaven' as Crooks later calls it, becomes the ambition not only of Lennie, but also spreads inadvertently to others – Candy, Crooks and Curley's wife. The recitation is Lennie's reward for being good. After killing Curley's wife he is tormented by the notion that he has destroyed his chances of living in this dream world.

15/92	Dreams
26/28	George
26/28	Lennie

28 George's voice became deeper.
Lennie and George are complementary characters and their relationship has a symmetry about it, as this section suggests. George has experience, wisdom and intelligence and can use such attributes to look after Lennie. Lennie, although limited by his simple intellect, has size and immense strength. Lennie is welcome at ranches because of his capacity for work; he is also a useful deterrent should anyone want to take advantage of George's lack of stature. This expression ('because I got you . . .') uttered familiarly by Lennie, seems to be a true assessment of their need for each other.

27/31	George
27/29	Lennie

29 They sat by the fire and filled . . .
We are made aware once more of Lennie's child-like nature. This small detail reminds us of an infant being fed.

28/31	Lennie

30 George motioned with his spoon again.
This arrangement will complete the symmetry of the novel as this is the location for its final events. It is particularly appropriate because of the way it is described as a haven of nature, a secret dream-like place, a 'pastoral idyll' – it suits Lennie's animal characteristics. The environment has a tranquillity and harmony, and this lessens the brutality of the eventual solution to George's dilemma. It is also interesting that in the Bible Adam,

26/31	Aspects of style
25/31	The natural world

after his tryst with Eve caused the downfall of Man, took refuge in a similar way from the wrath of God.

---

31 'You can jus' as well go to hell,' . . .
The first episode of the novel ends on a note of peace and harmony. As the light fails, the description is filled with appeals to our sense of hearing. Steinbeck has used this backdrop to add to the sense of a natural kinship between Lennie and George.

Section 2

Lennie and George arrive at the ranch.
Curley takes a dislike to Lennie.
Carlson suggests that Slim should give one of
his dog's puppies to Candy, and that
Candy's old dog should be put down.

Commentary

32 The bunk-house was a long, rectangular building.
This setting is composed with great care and no doubt is derived from Steinbeck's own experience as a ranch-hand. As with the novel's opening description, the writer's technique is theatrical, setting the scene first and then introducing characters through dialogue. Do you get the impression that it would be very easy to turn this novel into a film script? The exacting detail of the description certainly makes it easy to recreate accurately the bunk-house of Steinbeck's imagination. This 'home' for the workers is very sparse in comforts and contrasts harshly with the harmony of nature described in the novel's opening section.

31/37	Aspects of style
31/33	The natural world

33 'The boss was expectin' you last night,' . . .
These opening remarks by the old man establish the character of the boss before we meet him; they also contribute to our sense of unease at the immediately unfriendly environment which is full of discord. Lennie and George will have to endure living here.

0/35	The boss
32/34	The natural world

34 'The boss was expectin' you last night,' . . .
We are given a brief description of Candy. He is obviously an old ranch-hand who has been pensioned off. This incident gives us our first sketch of Candy, from which we begin to build a fuller picture as the novel progresses, and at the same time adds to the sense of intimidation in the environment. There is a suggestion that things are twisted, unnatural and unwelcoming, with the possibility of 'grey-backs' in the bedding. George's angry reaction to Candy reveals more about the boss and his attitude to the new workers. Steinbeck is working on our anticipation of trouble with this deliberate reiteration of the boss's actions. George needs a welcoming, friendly environment for Lennie's safety so this must surely make us apprehensive. Another ranch-hand is described as the 'stable buck', and is characterized as a 'nigger', indicating further prejudice and exploitation; like Candy he too has been deformed by an accident. There is an atmosphere of casual violence, which is no good for Lennie!

0/40	Candy
33/37	The natural world

35 George lifted his tick and looked . . .
This provides us with further information about the boss and anticipates his entrance into the novel. He vents his anger on the black stable-hand; provides the hands with whisky; and allows a fight between the crippled stable-hand and 'Smitty'. This all contributes to the atmosphere of latent violence and suggests a casual disregard for the usual standards of civilized behaviour.

33/36	The boss
0/41	Violence

36 Lennie was just finishing making his bed.
This description of the boss fits in with the pattern that Steinbeck has built up. His 'black' clothes remind us of the stereotyped 'good' and 'bad' men in westerns and the severity of his appearance is added to by the fact that he has a 'square steel buckle', rather than a more usual ornate one. He is a proud man, and wears 'high-heeled boots and spurs' to accentuate his

35/38	The boss

position. Our overall impression of him is unsympathetic and his nature would appear to be the very opposite to Lennie's mild, lumbering good-heartedness.

37 Lennie smiled to himself. 'Strong as a bull,' . . .
Again, Lennie is described in animal terms. This time the comparison emphasizes his great strength, but, of course, bulls also have a reputation for violence and sexuality. The allusion may be further evidence of George's unwitting revealing of the truth of things.

32/40	Aspects of style
31/46	Lennie
34/40	The natural world

38 George broke in loudly: . . .
This is a good example of George's caring and protective attitude towards Lennie. But is he over-protective, do you think? His constant interruptions here only serve to arouse suspicions in the boss's mind. He may well have attracted closer scrutiny than usual. What do you imagine might have been Lennie's reactions? Would he just have mumbled something idiotic or is he able to converse intelligently? Notice how he is quite articulate in the barn with Curley's wife, and in his 'internal discussions' at the end of the novel. Perhaps the only danger is that he might reveal something about the incident with the girl in Weed.

31/39	George
37/39	Lennie
36/0	The boss

39 When the sound of his footsteps . . .
George's comment that Lennie 'Damn near lost us the job' might seem rather a harsh judgment. Surely the opposite is true? It was George's extensive explanations that drew a more intense scrutiny from the boss. This might suggest that there is another dimension to the relationship between George and Lennie – does Lennie provide George with something on which to vent his exasperation when things are not going to plan? Does this help us to understand their relationship more fully – as outlined in the first paragraph of comment 24?

38/42	George
38/42	Lennie

40 The old man came slowly into the room.
There are unnatural elements in the bunk-house in the sense that the bunk-house environment is a contrast to that of the mountains and trees outside. This contrast is emphasized by such things as Candy's dog, which is at the end of its useful life, but has provided companionship for its gentle owner for many years. Notice how the dog's end neatly parallels the final actions of George and the death of Lennie.

37/46	Aspects of style
34/49	Candy
37/54	The natural world

41 'He's a nice fella,' the swamper agreed.
The first impression that Curley creates is complicated. His 'brown face', 'brown eyes' and 'tightly curled hair' belie the menace in his later conduct. His glance is cold and he naturally takes on the stance of a fighter, with his 'hands closed into fists'. Even the way he looks at Lennie and George is menacing. His 'work glove' on one hand is intriguing and, of course, his high-heeled cowboy boots give him a status above that of the work-hands.

0/43	Curley
35/43	Violence

42 'Let the big guy talk.'
This is the second confrontation caused by Lennie's adherence to George's advice to say nothing. Perhaps Curley has been put up to this provocation

39/50	George
39/46	Lennie

by his father, the boss. It would seem that Lennie's behaviour in remaining silent it going to attract interest and cause trouble.

43 Curley lashed his body around.
Notice how the menace and inherent viciousness of Curley extends even to the way in which he moves.

41/44   Curley
41/44   Violence

44 'We jus' come in,' said Lennie softly.
The stress here is on the violent nature of Curley's character and the fact that he has been a lightweight boxer, and is capable with his fists. The presence of such a character argues badly for the safety of Lennie and George.

43/45   Curley
43/45   Violence

45 The old man looked cautiously at the door . . .
Our awareness that the safety of Lennie is threatened is particularly heightened by this information. Curley obviously has what is called a 'Napoleon complex' – 'he's alla time picking scraps with big guys'. (The term originates in the suggestion that Napoleon Bonaparte's great successes in battle were in part attributable to his need to compensate, or make up for, his smallness of stature.) Since Lennie is a bear-like giant of a man, he seems certain to provoke a violent assault from Curley sooner or later. As is explained after this passage by Candy, from the point of view of his status, Curley cannot lose from such an assault.

44/47   Curley
44/50   Violence

46 George was watching the door.
We have not really been introduced to this aspect of Lennie's character before, but if Lennie 'don't know no rules' then he is potentially very dangerous indeed.

40/47   Aspects of
          style
42/47   Lennie

47 'Seems to me like he's worse lately,' . . .
Further information about Curley extends our knowledge of his character. He is proud of his new wife, particularly if it makes others envious – is this complementary to the fact that he is small? Notice the implication that his hand is kept soft by vaseline in order that he may 'pet' his wife. This petting is also a primary feature in Lennie's character. Steinbeck is seeding his narrative very carefully here; a confrontation between Lenne and Curley already looks inevitable.

46/49   Aspects of
          style
45/48   Curley
46/49   Lennie

48 'Well – she got the eye.'
Here is one suggestion to explain the way in which Curley is acting. If his wife is not satisfied with their relationship and marriage and is therefore looking around, then Curley's self-esteem and confidence will have been undermined. He might feel a very great need to establish his 'manliness' with the workers, but notice the way in which he goes about this. Why does a character like Slim not seem to need to establish his 'manliness' in the way Curley does? Why is it do you think, that Curley sees his stature or 'manliness' as something which is produced only by physically terrorizing others? Apart from the fact that we later learn that the ranch-hands despise him because of his aggressiveness, would his attitude have been more effective if he had possessed the physical stature of Lennie? Do the ranch-hands laugh at him mainly because he is small or because he is pugnacious? Notice how there is a kind of reverse relationship between the size and authority of characters in the novel and the extent of their aggressiveness.

47/55   Curley

49 'I seen her give Slim the eye.'
Curley's wife is pretty, and after only two weeks of marriage, has been observed giving Slim 'the eye', as well as others. Candy further believes Curley's wife to be a 'tart' and this has clear implications for us, when we consider the vulnerability of Lennie to such a woman. We have been prepared for this by Lennie's earlier references to 'girls' and the trouble in his last employment in Weed. Why do you think it could be that a 'tart' might be an especially explosive kind of woman to have around Lennie? How might Lennie interpret such a woman's behaviour? Do the other ranch-hands interpret the behaviour of Curley's wife in this way?

50 George stared at his solitaire lay . . .
George has read the situation correctly and with intelligence. He is frightened for Lennie's safety not only because of Curley's fighting disposition, but also because of the way Curley's wife is likely to flaunt her attractiveness.

Incidentally, notice how the subtle use of George's solitaire card game acts as a premonition of the future – one of the novel's themes is loneliness.

51 Lennie's eyes were frightened.
Despite his immense strength and size, Lennie is clearly terrified of violence. He is not conscious of his own capabilities.

52 'Sure, George. I ain't gonna say a word.'
The unfriendliness of this environment is echoed by the harsh and abrasive noises.

53 Both men glanced up . . .
The extravagance and unsuitable nature of her outfit adds up to an unsympathetic description. She has 'rouged lips', 'eyes, heavily made up', and her 'fingernails were red'. Her hair hangs in 'sausages' and her voice has a 'nasal, brittle quality'. This is hardly a romantic portrait and her general appearance seems unsuitable for life on a ranch. The dominating colour of red is the symbolic colour of ladies of loose morals, as in the common expression 'a scarlet woman'.

54 George looked away from her and then back.
Even the posture of Curley's wife against the door frame is designed to provoke sexual interest. She seems very conscious of herself. Nothing in what we are told directly about her intentions suggests that she is being sexually provocative. What is it then that makes us so sure that this is the case? (The word 'bridled' will help you here.) Lennie is clearly impressed with the animal-like display by Curley's wife. Notice how this is yet another example of the way various elements of the ranch environment are piecing together to form an inescapable trap for Lennie. Do you think Lennie could have escaped?

55 She was suddenly apprehensive.
On learning that Curley has gone home looking for her, she becomes nervous. This suggests that there has been some sort of tension between them. What do you suspect it might have been about? The implication so far

Characters and ideas
previous/next comment

47/52	Aspects of style
40/93	Candy
0/53	Curley's wife
47/51	Lennie
42/57	George
45/51	Violence
49/54	Lennie
50/55	Violence
49/53	Aspects of style
52/54	Aspects of style
49/54	Curley's wife
53/62	Aspects of style
53/55	Curley's wife
51/56	Lennie
40/56	The natural world
48/66	Curley
54/56	Curley's wife
51/58	Violence

is that her behaviour during the two weeks of marriage and her over-familiar contact with the ranch-hands could be the cause. Do you think she is frightened of Curley? If she is, why does she behave the way she does – isn't she deliberately courting disaster? Or is she unwittingly provocative and ignorant of the effects of her behaviour?

56 'She's purty,' said Lennie defensively.
Disaster! The uncomplicated, bovine Lennie is deeply impressed by the obvious 'prettiness' of Curley's wife and he is transfixed. Whereas the others can see the limitations of her attractions and are able to speculate unflatteringly about her morals, Lennie is only conscious of her animal awareness of the opposite sex. He seems to see her, appropriately given that she is wearing so much red, as an animal in heat.

55/57	Curley's wife
54/58	Lennie
54/66	The natural world

57 'Listen to me, you crazy bastard,' . . .
George senses imminent danger and tries to warn Lennie about the type of woman that Curley's wife represents. He has experience of women like her, but stresses that she is one of the most dangerous of her type. Notice how he calls her 'jail bait', although in fact the consequences of her actions and appearance are far worse than any jail sentence.

| 56/66 | Curley's wife |
| 50/58 | George |

58 Lennie tried to disengage his ear.
Lennie intuitively senses trouble and wants to escape. Despite his slow-witted nature, he seems able to see through to the truth of the matter and seems to have an innate good sense. Perhaps he has an animal's gift for perceiving trouble. But for George the desirability of escape has to be weighed against the possibility of financial gain; his quest for riches overrides his wisdom. His hesitation costs him dearly.

57/60	George
56/60	Lennie
56/62	The natural world
55/60	Violence

59 A tall man stood in the doorway.
This passage introduces Slim – a character who is sympathetically drawn by Steinbeck. He is a man of 'majesty' and 'authority', and he is capable 'of understanding beyond thought'. This treatment points him out to us as a character of strong moral principles whose role will be to act as mediator and counsellor in the events to come. His is the calm voice of reason.

| 0/60 | Slim |

60 He smoothed out his crushed hat . . .
Slim's tone throughout these exchanges is in marked contrast to the harshness of the rest of the ranch and its brutal inhabitants. He speaks 'gently', and 'his tone was friendly'. Notice how, unlike many others in the novel, he is not suspicious of the relationship between George and Lennie and he gives tacit approval to their relationship. He sees them as having complementary natures. Whereas people like the boss and Curley have reacted aggressively to the pair, Slim wants them to work on his team. As he is a 'master craftsman' this is a generous gesture. He illustrates that you can command respect through natural authority rather than through bullying and violence.

0/64	Authority
58/61	George
58/61	Lennie
59/64	Slim
58/66	Violence

61 'Sure,' said George. 'We kinda look . . .'
This is a further example of the mutual support which George and Lennie offer each other.

| 60/71 | George |
| 60/65 | Lennie |

62 A powerful, big-stomached man . . .
This introduction to Carlson demonstrates his cheerful good humour. He
seems to be friendly with Slim. His question about Slim's dog reminds us of
George's promise of a pup to Lennie. After allowing the narrative to pause
for the introduction of the rest of the characters, the appearance of Carlson
moves it firmly forward. Notice Steinbeck's impressive economy in the use
of dramatic devices to bring the novel to its tragic end – the number of key
incidents is remarkably few. Try to establish for yourself how few incidents
you think are enough to make the novel's eventual outcome inevitable.

63 Carlson said thoughtfully: . . .
Carlson is unsentimental in the way that he suggests that the dog should be
destroyed; he sees that it has no further usefulness. His suggestion is
practical, but does not really take account of the strong bond between Candy
and his pet. Even at this early point, you might feel that you are aware of a
strongly underlined parallel here – between Candy's loneliness and the
comfort afforded him by his dog, and the relationship between George and
Lennie.

64 Slim stood up slowly and with dignity.
It is interesting that Slim does not respond directly to Carlson's suggestion
about the dog. We get the impression that he will give the proposition
careful thought. Why do you think he did not answer right away? Notice
how his delay adds suspense and therefore tension to the coming debate
with Candy, because we are still unsure how the decision will come out. If
Slim had voiced his opinion at this moment, would we still have felt that the
eventual fate of Candy's dog was firmly decided, or as yet still in the
balance? Notice how Slim moves 'with dignity' and shows concern for the
welfare of Lennie and George.

65 Lennie was watching George excitedly.
Lennie is overjoyed at the possibility of owning a puppy and George,
perhaps sensing a kind of solution to the tensions that he has observed,
proposes to ask Slim for one of his.

66 'You seen a girl around here?'
From his behaviour it is obvious that Curley is spoiling for a fight. Notice
how he sizes George up during their conversation. He is almost always
angry and appears to spend quite a bit of time checking on his wife's
movements. In this novel Steinbeck does not allow any sense of security to
last for long and this threatening episode interrupts Lennie's delight at the
prospect of owning a puppy. Curley's appearance, and his mean conduct,
remind us that trouble is not far away.

Characters and ideas	
previous/next comment	
54/63	Aspects of style
0/63	Carlson
58/65	The natural world
62/67	Aspects of style
62/79	Carlson
0/73	Loneliness
60/82	Authority
60/68	Slim
61/69	Lennie
62/66	The natural world
0/114	Curley
57/76	Curley's wife
65/68	The natural world
60/70	Violence

Section 3

*The setting is in the bunkhouse.
Candy's dog is killed. George and Lennie
draw Candy into their dream of a place of
their own. Curley picks a fight with Lennie
and has his hand crushed.*

Commentary

Characters and ideas
previous/next comment

67 Although there was evening brightness showing . . .

In keeping with the rest of the novel this section opens with a short piece of environmental description which includes the harsher sounds of the 'thuds' and 'clays' of the horseshoe game. The 'evening brightness' so beautifully described in the first section is noticeably excluded from this scene, and the atmosphere in the bunk-house is now 'dusk'. This change of mood maintains the sense of an unfriendly environment, and provides the setting for the next important piece of extended action.

63/69 Aspects of style

68 'It wasn't nothing,' said Slim.

Slim has agreed to let Lennie have one of the puppies. It is characteristic of him that he makes little of the gift. Interestingly, we learn that Slim killed several of the puppies at birth. The reason why this is interesting is that it was accepted by everybody as quite normal behaviour, and yet the killing by Lennie of his puppy has wholly different interpretations. Why should it be that Slim's deliberate drowning of *several* puppies is unworthy of comment (even by Lennie) and yet the accidental killing of *one* by Lennie is a catalyst for the final tragedy? (Hint: think about whether the two characters knew what they were doing at the time. Consider how this affected the way they themselves reacted to what they had done.)

64/70 Slim
66/69 The natural world

69 George said: 'It wasn't much to you, maybe . . .'

George describes Lennie's delight when he has been given the puppy. The description adds welcome comedy to the novel with the suggestion that Lennie will climb into the box with the pups.

Notice how Steinbeck constantly uses hints and premonitions of disaster. Hardly a page goes by without some reference to Lennie's attraction for trouble – when he plays with mice George reminds him about the girl in Weed whom he molested, and we eventually see the dead mouse replaced by a dead puppy. Added to this we have George's observation that Lennie seems to get into trouble 'like you always done before'. Also there is Curley, who threatens violence every time we see him, and there is the presence of his wife, who is described as 'jail bait'. The overall effect is that disaster is imminent, and is hanging, sword-like, over George and Lennie.

67/71 Aspects of style
65/70 Lennie
68/77 The natural world

70 'It wasn't nothing,' Slim repeated.

This not only illustrates a facet of Lennie's character but also prepares us for the bewilderment he experiences when attacked by Curley. This emphasis on Lennie's strength not only demonstrates Slim's generosity in praising him but also serves to prepare us for the violence of this section by reminding us of Lennie's capabilities: 'he damn near killed his partner'.

69/71 Lennie
68/72 Slim
66/73 Violence

71 Slim moved back slightly so the light . . .

Having created the sympathetic character of Slim, Steinbeck uses a dramatic device to reveal more about the relationship before the story continues. By way of conversation George can relate to us, too, the circumstances which brought this unlikely combination together: their origin in Auburn; Aunt Clara; the need for companionship. More is also revealed about Lennie's

69/85 Aspects of style
61/85 George
70/72 Lennie

character and the absolute trust that he has in George, together with his
sometimes frighteningly unreasoned obedience.

72 'He's a nice fella,' said Slim.
Slim's readiness to praise Lennie shows not only his thoughtfulness, but
also illustrates once more the generosity in his character. He sees Lennie's
true worth.

71/73	Lennie
70/73	Slim

73 George stacked the scattered cards . . .
There is plenty of violence in the environment of this ranch and 'meanness'
is bred, according to Slim, by isolation. We learn that George has no
relations and has been saved from loneliness and eventual bitterness by
Lennie. Loneliness and isolation become a preoccupying theme of the novel
from this point onwards; they are used to highlight the plight of the itinerant
worker who goes through life without base or roots. How far do you think
this explains the reason for George and Lennie's partnership?

71/80	George
71/81	Lennie
63/79	Loneliness
72/74	Slim
70/75	Violence

74 'He ain't mean,' said Slim.
Slim's assessment of situations is like the word of God. No doubt George is
proud that Lennie's true worth has been noted in Slim's eyes.

73/75	Lennie
73/76	Slim

75 'Well, he seen this girl in a red dress.'
This explanation by George provides us with more information about the
incident in Weed which led to their flight from their last job. The serious
nature of the offence is underlined by the fact that Lennie would have been
'lynched' had they caught him.

Look at how we are being prepared for such events by the colour of the girl's
dress – red – which is the dominating colour in the appearance of Curley's
wife. Additionally we are prepared for the way in which Lennie 'innocently'
inflicts injury on Curley because of his panic.

71/79	Aspects of style
74/76	Lennie
73/90	Violence

76 Slim's eyes were level and unwinking.
Slim is contemplating the evidence being given by George about Lennie's
actions. He believes George's assertion that Lennie is not dangerous and had
not intended to harm the girl. However, we are witnessing an escalation in
the behaviour of Lennie and, clearly, he was fascinated by the blatant
sexuality of Curley's wife. Whether such a state of innocence will survive
given this kind of provocation is hard to predict, and it returns us to the
question of the motivation for Lennie's 'petting'. Why does Lennie need to
'pet' things do you think?

66/89	Curley's wife
75/77	Lennie
74/78	Slim

77 Lennie came in through the door.
This episode illustrates the limitation of Lennie's understanding, in that he
puts the puppy at risk by removing it from its mother. It shows us just how
powerful his urge for 'petting' is and how much it appears to dominate his
personality. Does Lennie ever consider any of the consequences of his
actions? There is a lot of evidence to say that he does not – remember the way
he drinks water at the beginning of the book – but is there any to argue that
he is actually able to see the implications of what he does?

76/78	Lennie
69/79	The natural world

78 Slim had not moved.
Notice Slim's appraisal of the situation. Does he perhaps seriously

77/81	Lennie

underestimate the harm which might befall Lennie as a result of his needs and his immense strength?

76/83	Slim

79 The thick-bodied Carlson came in . . .

With the return of Carlson to the bunk-house we move into the next important episode in the novel. Carlson has prepared the ground for this move already and has, of course, primed Slim. Candy and the dog have been together so long that Candy is not aware of the smell that surrounds his companion. Carlson says, 'he ain't no good to himself' as a justification for killing him. How far do you think that this relationship later parallels that of George and Lennie? Notice how the way Carlson talks about Candy's dog is a mirror of how the stable buck Crooks thinks the ranch-hands treat him.

75/84	Aspects of style
63/80	Carlson
73/92	Loneliness
77/80	The natural world

80 George said: 'I seen a guy in Weed that . . .'

Unwittingly, in dealing specifically with how to shoot the dog painlessly in terms of the exact location for the bullet, Carlson is teaching George how to dispose of Lennie humanely. Is Carlson's detachment and cool analysis of the situation, though harsh, probably justified?

79/81	Carlson
73/81	George
79/81	The natural world

81 'Well, you ain't bein' kind to him . . .'

These are dreadful words to hear spoken about an old pet. Applied here to the dog they are apt, and are all part of Carlson's strategy, but, ironically, he is at the same time sentencing Lennie, who will later suffer the same fate. In one sense the death of the dog has less finality because there is comfort in the gift of the new puppy to Candy.

80/82	Carlson
80/85	George
78/83	Lennie
80/83	The natural world

Candy and his dog are an obvious parallel to George and Lennie, even to the way the dog follows Candy like Lennie follows George. Notice also that just as Candy feels trapped by his relationship with his dog, so George feels trapped by his responsibilities for Lennie. Is there a clue here to the basic reason for the loneliness of the ranch-hands, that they shy away from any real commitment and responsibility? Would this be a fair judgment on every character in the book, do you think?

Notice how Lennie is eventually shot by the same gun, and in the same place, as Candy's dog. These 'echoing' devices give a strong sense of unity to the book.

82 'Well, you ain't bein' kind to him . . .'

Carlson obviously takes pride in the way in which he would dispose of the animal. In demonstrating his competence he is unwittingly educating George.

64/83	Authority
81/85	Carlson

83 The skinner had been studying the old dog . . .

Slim's opinions are valued by all the ranchers, and such a pronouncement, seen as a final judgment, seals the dog's fate. By appealing to others to do the same for him should he 'get old and a cripple', Slim paves the way for the gun to be used on Lennie, who is mentally 'crippled'. His considered verdict has the force of law.

82/85	Authority
81/88	Lennie
78/94	Slim
81/84	The natural world

84 Candy looked for help from face to face.

The character of Whit remains relatively undrawn. This episode interrupts the main narrative, slows down the pace of the action and contributes to the

79/85	Aspects of style

	Characters and ideas previous/next comment

suspense generated by the proposal to shoot the dog. The excitement shown by Whit over the appearance of an acquaintance's name in a pulp magazine serves to illustrate the poverty of experience and education in some ranch-hands.

83/88	The natural world
0/87	Whit

85 'The hell I ain't. Got a Luger.'
Carlson is not a cowboy, but does possess a gun – not the traditional Colt but a German pistol. The significance of this exchange is that it indicates to George where the gun is kept.

84/86	Aspects of style
83/93	Authority
82/93	Carlson
81/91	George

86 'Take a shovel,' said Slim shortly.
The shooting of the dog contrasts with the shooting of Lennie in the length of time that it takes. Notice how Steinbeck, by using muted sounds, like 'shuffle', 'rippled', 'snapping', 'gnawing' and eventually 'shot', emphasizes the tension and the silence in the bunk-house.

85/87	Aspects of style

87 Whit broke out: 'What the hell's . . .'
The character of Whit is again used to slow down the action and in this case it provides relief from the oppressive tension of the bunk-house as the men await a sign that the dog has been shot. Whit represents the normal, average farm-hand.

86/90	Aspects of style
84/92	Whit

88 'That big new guy's messin' around with your pups . . .'
Immediately after the dog's demise we are reminded of Lennie and his weaknesses. George's words a few lines further on: 'If that crazy bastard's foolin' around . . .' ring with double meaning, for the words 'foolin' around' are normally applied to intimate behaviour between males and females in America.

83/106	Lennie
84/89	The natural world

89 Slim followed the stable buck out of the room.
Whit uses the name of Slim's dog – Lulu – to describe Curley's wife. This is appropriate, given the recent condition that the bitch was in! His description of her 'concealing nothing' and giving everyone the 'eye', coming straight after the description of Lennie's behaviour with the dogs in the barn, emphasizes Lennie's innate ability to get into trouble.

76/90	Curley's wife
88/96	The natural world

90 It was obvious that Whit was not . . .
It is important to the plot that there is a general expectation of trouble amongst the ranch-hands and Curley. George and Lennie's employment is most inopportune; they have arrived at the ranch at a time when trouble really is imminent. Steinbeck builds towards a climax which will fuse all these different elements together.

87/93	Aspects of style
66/94	Curley
89/91	Curley's wife
75/95	Violence

91 George said: 'She's gonna make a mess.'
George is particularly conscious of the potential trouble that lies in Curley's wife's behaviour. So why doesn't he move out straight away?

90/122	Curley's wife
27/98	Dreams
27/98	George

92 Whit said: 'If you got idears . . .'
Whit underlines the predicament of the itinerant worker. Their existence is
mean and centres around violence, cheap sex, drinking and fighting. They
earn insufficient money to get ahead and build up a 'stake' for a more deeply
satisfying life. It is interesting to note that a prostitute is suggested as a
reasonable alternative to Curley's wife. Why do you think it is that the men
are unable to amass sufficient money for a 'stake'? Why is it that they always
spend it on 'blackjack' and 'whores', as Crooks observes? Consider to what
extent their desire for carefree enjoyment and pleasure is the serpent in their
Garden of Eden.

79/104	Loneliness
87/97	Whit

93 'Well, a guy got to have some fun sometime,' . . .
Carlson may be practical and have the cold nerve necessary to kill the dog,
but he is fairly callous too. He makes no effort to conceal the cleaning of the
recently fired gun from Candy, who we feel must find the snapping of the
ejector a painful reminder of his dog's death. However, Steinbeck does need
to draw attention to the gun's existence, because the resolution of the plot
depends upon it.

90/99	Aspects of style
85/94	Authority
49/102	Candy
85/99	Carlson

The killing of the dog is an interesting example of the technique which
Steinbeck was trying out in *Of Mice and Men*, which was a cross between a
novel and a play or drama. Each of the six sections (actually split into
chapters in some editions) deals with one scene. Each opens with a
description of the scene and is followed by dialogue between characters who
enter and exit in the same way that they would in a play or film. If you look
carefully you will notice that almost every piece of description or story-
telling is like a stage direction to a theatre director. Each section (or chapter)
could easily be translated into an act or scene on a stage and, indeed, when
the book was first performed as a play (in November 1937) the dialogue was
changed very little. Another thing which reminds us of a play script is that
very few characters are used – far less than in most novels.

How effective is Steinbeck's play/novel technique, do you think? Why do
you think he experimented with this way of writing? Think about how
effective his method is in getting the reader to imagine the events and the
conversation which take place, and how easy it is to follow what is going
on – do you think it works better than the more traditionally written novel?

Many novels which are now highly regarded were written before the
widespread availability of films and television. You may have read some
such works, probably with great enjoyment. But the invention of film and
television sometimes changed the way drama was made to work. You can
reread interesting parts of a good novel, but it is more difficult to look back
over parts of a film or a theatre production. Do you think Steinbeck may
have written *Of Mice and Men* in the way he did because of changes in the
nature of the media? Think about when the book was written.

94 'She ain't been here,' said Whit.
Presumably Curley, too, recognizes in Slim something different and
superior, and sees him as a rival for the affections of his wife.

93/99	Authority
90/95	Curley
83/96	Slim

95 Curley looked threateningly . . .
Curley is looking for a fight and a victim on whom to vent his frustration and
anger. This is menacing because he has been a boxer of some ability.

94/105	Curley
90/97	Violence

Characters and ideas previous/next comment		

96 'Went out in the barn,' said George.
Slim is a mysterious and potentially dangerous member of the group. This maintains the sense of authority that he contributes to the events. This action by Slim supports our impression of his competence in his work and his genuinely caring nature. He has made a special point of coping with the horse's injury himself.

| 94/97 | Slim |
| 89/101 | The natural world |

97 Whit stood up. 'I guess maybe . . .'
As a typical ranch-hand, Whit is eager to participate in any brawling, and urges George to go and witness the confrontation. It is suggested that it is unthinkable that Slim will have tangled with Curley's wife, and so an argument, at least, seems inevitable.

96/105	Slim
95/105	Violence
92/0	Whit

98 George said: 'I'm stayin' right here.'
George wants to keep out of trouble and avoid getting the sack. The choice between avoiding trouble by going away and staying to earn a 'stake' becomes increasingly important. George is torn between the need for Lennie's safety and the possible realization of his dream of a homestead. He wants more than the Whits and Carlsons of the ranch-hand world – he has clear and definite ambitions.

| 91/100 | Dreams |
| 91/100 | George |

99 Carlson finished the cleaning of the gun . . .
The location of the gun is important to the development of the plot, and it is therefore witnessed by George.

93/103	Aspects of style
94/118	Authority
93/107	Carlson

100 'No. She never come.'
George appears to have a very biased view of women and sees them as instruments to relieve certain basic urges, as a device to 'get ever'thing outa his system all at once, an' no messes'. He does not express the need for any companionship beyond this and his lack of trust is further illustrated by the fact that women do not feature in his dream of a smallholding. Does this also illustrate a fear of real relationships on his part, do you think?

| 98/101 | Dreams |
| 98/101 | George |

101 Lennie drummed on the table . . .
This dream-like speculation of George slows down the pace of the novel and provides a period of 'pastoral' calm before the storm. The life and surroundings he describes are the very opposite of his present experience, moving as he does between farm and farm for seasonal work. His life, and Lennie's, would be more closely related to nature – as he says 'when we put in a crop, why we'd be there to take the crop up'. The circle of nature would be complete. The situation sounds so much like an idyll that it comes as some surprise to us that the place does in fact exist and is not just a fantasy fairy-tale concocted to amuse Lennie. This makes the urgent need for a 'stake' more easily understood.

100/102	Dreams
100/102	George
96/106	The natural world

Man's longing for the land is a favourite theme of Steinbeck's, and he returned to it in nearly every novel he wrote. Although we can see several examples of personal tragedy in *Of Mice and Men*, Steinbeck clearly meant the story also to be a parable of the human condition – as the novel's final title indicates. In the poem from which the title is taken, Burns wrote that 'the best laid schemes o' mice an' men gang aft a-gley'. The phrase '. . . gang aft a-gley' literally means 'go often astray', but Steinbeck does not translate

Burns' 'aft' as 'often', but as 'always'. Notice how in *Of Mice and Men* Crooks says 'Nobody never gets to heaven, and nobody gets no land.' Similarly George says at the end that 'I think I knowed from the very first. I think I knowed we'd never do her'.

Notice how Crooks uses double negatives when he says, 'Nobody never gets to heaven, and nobody gets no land'. Although we understand him to mean nobody *ever* gets to heaven and nobody ever gets *any* land, it is interesting to see that what he actually says is that everybody gets to heaven and everybody gets some land. This can be seen either as an unconscious revelation of the inner desires of many of the itinerant workers or as a piece of bitter irony on Steinbeck's part – for Lennie does indeed get to heaven by the end of the book and the land he gets is his grave.

102 George sat entranced with his own picture.

At this point, George suddenly realizes that what has been a distant dream is now reality, with Candy's involvement and contribution. It offers them all self-respect and companionship and it is typical of Steinbeck that he offers his characters such hope before plunging them into dreadful turmoil. It is a very harsh twist of the plot to have allowed them to get so near to their goal.

93/103	Candy
101/104	Dreams
101/106	George

103 Candy sat on the edge of his bunk.

Candy is nearing the end of his useful life and unwittingly expresses a desire which foreshadows Lennie's death.

| 99/121 | Aspects of style |
| 102/106 | Candy |

104 George stood up. 'We'll do her,' he said.

This shared state of euphoria and sense of beauty contrast very starkly with the surroundings of the ranch that they are on. They have suddenly been offered an alternative to their normal expectation, thanks to Candy's offer.

| 102/112 | Dreams |
| 92/136 | Loneliness |

105 Voices were approaching from outside.

Curley's suspicions are unfounded and there has been a confrontation which has resulted in Curley being compromised. This can only serve to increase Curley's humiliation and therefore frustration and anger. In this way we are moving towards the inevitable clash between Curley and Lennie, as Lennie has no defence comparable to that of Slim or Carlson.

95/108	Curley
97/119	Slim
97/107	Violence

106 'I ought to of shot that dog myself, . . .'

These words of Candy bring to an end the pastoral idyll and the hopeful note of an attainable alternative life. At the end of the novel George has to take the initiative and shoot Lennie before Curley's shot kills him in a painful, long and drawn-out way. George's dilemma is similar to that of Candy's, although of much greater severity, but he has the courage to see the grotesque event through.

103/110	Candy
102/116	George
88/112	Lennie
101/113	The natural world

107 'Why'n't you tell her to stay the hell home . . .'

Carlson is outspoken and enjoys interfering with everyone's problems. His advice here only serves to aggravate Curley's already rising temper, with devastating results for Lennie.

| 99/109 | Carlson |
| 105/108 | Violence |

108 Curley whirled on Carlson.

The way in which Curley moves from man to man, tolerating the jibes and

| 105/111 | Curley |

humiliation of their comments, indicates that Carlson's assessment of his character is probably true. He does appear to be cowardly, despite his notoriously violent streak.

107/109	Violence

109 Carlson laughed.

Carlson appears to enjoy making the situation with Curley worse. His words are calculated to inflame matters. Carlson is a trouble-maker who enjoys this kind of situation because he is confident of his ability to handle any resulting violence.

107/207	Carlson
108/110	Violence

110 Candy joined the attack with joy.

Candy, although one-handed, is in the company of George, Slim and Carlson, and is therefore safe from attack. Notice how he takes a delight in goading Curley further. Unfortunately this leaves Lennie open as an alternative target.

106/130	Candy
109/111	Violence

111 Curley stepped over to Lennie like a terrier.

All of Curley's appearances in the novel have prepared us for this confrontation. He has become increasingly animated and it is characteristic that he should pick on Lennie for his display of violence. Ironically, in picking on the large but gentle Lennie, he is demonstrating his own cowardice.

108/112	Curley
110/113	Violence

112 Then Curley's rage exploded.

There is a dreadful irony in the fact that Lennie's continuing thoughts about his imminently rosy future on the ranch should lead to his downfall, as his smile is misinterpreted by Curley.

111/114	Curley
104/121	Dreams
106/113	Lennie

113 Lennie looked helplessly at George . . .

Despite his size Lennie has two distinct disadvantages: he will not act unless commanded to by George and he is terrified by aggression. Because of these characteristics he does not make any attempt to defend himself.

112/116	Lennie
106/114	The natural world
111/115	Violence

114 Lennie looked helplessly at George . . .

Notice the use of animal images here: 'the dirty little rat'. If Lennie is a 'bear', then Curley is the rat.

112/115	Curley
113/116	The natural world

115 George was on his feet yelling: . . .

Curley is an unfair fighter and is obviously out to inflict grave damage.

114/119	Curley
113/125	Violence

116 George was on his feet yelling: . . .

Lennie needs George to 'trigger' his actions. We are reminded of the earlier description of Lennie being bear-like by his 'paws' and posture.

106/108	George
113/117	Lennie
114/123	The natural world

117 Curley's fist was swinging when . . .
Steinbeck has carefully and economically provided us with clues that would enable us to predict Lennie's action. Lennie's immense strength and tenacity crush Curley's hand. It is not an aggressive act but more of a reflex; it is a defensive move similar to that of the bear, which constrains by hugging – a sort of deadly embrace!

116/118   Lennie

118 Suddenly Lennie let go his hold.
This demonstrates the extent of the responsibility George has for Lennie's actions. Lennie is almost uncontrollable, and it takes a great deal of effort from George to penetrate Lennie's fear to first of all get him to act defensively, and secondly to get him to release his grasp.

99/119   Authority
116/121   George
117/119   Lennie

As you read the book you may be struck by the number of times Steinbeck refers, in one way or another, to hands. In fact the word is used well over one hundred times and its frequency is a little puzzling; Steinbeck sometimes seems to go out of his way unnecessarily to use the word. On one level its frequent use is fairly clear and straightforward, as when Lennie's hands are called 'paws'; Candy has a hand missing; Curley keeps one hand in a glove full of vaseline; Crooks's palms are mentioned as being pink; George has 'small, strong hands'; Slim's hands are 'delicate in their action as those of a temple dancer'; and Curley's wife has hands which are described only in terms of fingers and red fingernails.

However, this fails to account for why Steinbeck dwells on most of the seemingly deliberate uses of the word. For example, although Curley is 'handy' and Lennie 'ain't handy' the description of the fight relies heavily on the use of hand imagery. Sometimes the characters' hands seem to have a life of their own, as when Lennie's 'hands went into the pocket again' and when his 'closed hand slowly obeyed'. Later on George 'looked at his right hand that had thrown the gun away' and Slim 'subdued one hand with the other and held it down'. Interestingly enough, the use of the word 'hand' to describe a common agricultural worker is extremely rare in the book.

Consider to what extent this dehumanizing of individuals into physical parts, rather than whole people, contributes to one of the main points of the book: that the characters are lonely, incomplete people in search of a way to become whole.

119 Curley sat down on the floor, . . .
We have become accustomed to regarding Slim as a man of integrity, truth and firmness. His views are 'law'. His surprise and horror give greater emphasis to Lennie's strength and the damage of which he is capable. Although Curley's provocation has resulted in his getting a just punishment, Slim still has enough compassion to care for Curley once he is injured, and, despite the fact that he too had been abused by Curley before the fight, Slim has the natural authority to take charge of his welfare.

118/120   Authority
115/120   Curley
118/122   Lennie
105/120   Slim

120 Slim said: 'Carlson . . .'
Slim is definitely in control of the situation and also has the intelligence to manipulate the events for George and Lennie's benefit. He turns Curley's pride against him, and suggests that if the truth were known, then Curley would be an object of derision.

119/152   Authority
119/159   Curley
119/152   Slim

121 George said: 'Slim, will we get canned now?'
It is George's single-minded pursuit of the 'stake', in disregard of the hostility of the environment and its probable consequences for Lennie, that leads to the tragic resolution of the story. Half his fears have already come true – the situation has provoked the fight, and we still have Curley's wife to contend with.

122 George broke in: 'Lennie was jus' scairt,' . . .
It does not matter to whom George told this. The point is that in any situation that causes Lennie to panic, like a bear, he hangs on. From the point of view of the story, we have only dealt with one aspect of the possible problems on the ranch, that Lennie has tangled with Curley. What will happen if the same reaction is triggered off with Curley's wife?

123 'I can still tend the rabbits, George?'
Lennie is unable to discriminate between right and wrong – he has only an animal's sense of protection. The prospect of 'tending the rabbits' acts as a moral register, although Lennie is, confusingly, an amoral character – he has only intuition to guide him.

Characters and ideas	
previous/next comment	
103/124	Aspects of style
112/123	Dreams
118/130	George
91/158	Curley's wife
119/123	Lennie
121/133	Dreams
122/130	Lennie
116/129	The natural world

Section 4

*This section, set in the harness room of
the barn, brings together the dreams
of the men for a place of their own and
the temptation and catalyst of
Curley's wife. She destroys their budding
friendships and poisons the dream.*

Commentary

124 Crooks, the negro stable buck, . . .
Section four opens with a carefully detailed description of the harness room of the stables, which serves the same dramatic purpose of creating a setting as has been observed in the other sections. Notice how easy it would be to construct and decorate a stage set from the instructions given. These descriptions which introduce each section are probably derived from Steinbeck's own experience. The neat, workman-like impression of the place is an effect of the detail Steinbeck concentrates on, and gives us a good indication that Crooks, who lives in the room, has a committed and professional attitude towards his charges, the horses.

125 Crooks, the negro stable buck, . . .
Crooks, as his name suggests, was 'crooked' in the spine as the result of an accident. Notice how this fact makes the final comment of this episode particularly ironic (where Crooks returns to putting liniment on his back). He is less of an itinerant worker than some of the others, and this room represents 'home'.

126 Crooks possessed several pairs of shoes . . .
No doubt Crooks is supposed to be exceptional in that he is literate and conscious of his rights—notice how he had 'a mauled copy of the California civil code for 1905'. Notice also how 'large gold-rimmed spectacles' are prominent above his bed. These are symbols of his learning.

127 This room was swept and fairly neat . . .
Crooks is 'proud and aloof', unusual for a black in America in the thirties, and he has a strength of character which demands respect. He has eyes which 'glitter with intensity', and his 'deep black wrinkles' and 'pain-tightened lips' seem to indicate long hours of silent suffering.

128 Crooks sat on his bunk.
Crooks is in constant pain and treats himself as he would the horses, with liniment. It is a private act of a private man and he is understandably annoyed at the interruption from Lennie.

129 Noiselessly, Lennie appeared in . . .
Crooks is isolated and solitary and does not welcome intrusions into his privacy. His 'scowl' can be attributed to his pride. Much of Crook's pride and truculence is his defence against the harsh treatment he has endured from the work-hands. He has been rejected by the inhabitants of the bunk-house because of his colour. Notice how he also says 'they say I stink', which must remind us of Carlson's remarks about Candy's dog. From what he reveals about the treatment he has received it would seem that his attitude is justified, and that he has little reason to trust Lennie.

Characters and ideas previous/next comment	
121/130	Aspects of style
0/125	Crooks
124/126	Crooks
115/129	Violence
125/127	Crooks
126/128	Crooks
127/129	Crooks
128/130	Crooks
123/131	The natural world
125/134	Violence

130 Noiselessly, Lennie appeared in . . .
In view of recent events it might strike us as being very foolhardy of George not to keep an eye on Lennie. Why then does he get left alone? Think about this event from the author's point of view. For Steinbeck, it was essential to get rid of most of the hands, to allow the physical cripples (Crooks and Candy), and the mental cripple (Lennie) to get together without fear of interruption. Why do you think Steinbeck might have wanted these characters collected together like this? Look at what they talk about. Consider what we learn about each of the men and ask yourself what this tells us about the dreams and aspirations of the ranch-hands and itinerant workers of the time. If you ignore, for a moment, their particular circumstances, do you think their hopes and dreams are peculiar to their time and country, or do you feel that they are common to most people?

124/137	Aspects of style
110/133	Candy
129/131	Crooks
121/138	George
123/132	Lennie

131 'Well, I got a right to have a light.'
Crooks has a knowledge of, and interest in, animals and is drawn by Steinbeck with considerable sympathy.

130/132	Crooks
129/133	The natural world

132 'Why ain't you wanted?' Lennie asked.
Lennie's attitude gives Crooks little reason to be antagonized. His usual defence against the white ranch-hands is to remain 'aloof', but he sees in Lennie a genuine, uncomplicated and open nature that offers friendship without prejudice. Crook's tone becomes 'a little more friendly' as he gradually perceives that Lennie is no threat. But later on in this episode Lennie seems to become considerably threatening. Is Lennie unpredictable? Under what kinds of circumstance does he become threatening?

131/134	Crooks
130/135	Lennie

133 'All but old Candy. He just sets . . .'
Candy has remained at the ranch, excited by the prospects that the new farm has opened up. He sees the offer as an escape from the depressing finality of the ranch and preoccupies himself by planning for the future. George has suggested that Candy should take care of Lennie at the farm, and he has taken the offer very seriously. Having this protective job to do also helps him to cope with the grief occasioned by the loss of his dog.

130/148	Candy
123/135	Dreams
131/140	The natural world

134 'Jus' nuts,' said Crooks. 'I don't blame the guy . . .'
George's intention is to get Lennie out of harm's way rather than sight. The unkindness of Crooks stems from the opportunity to display a superior intellect for once, without danger.

132/135	Crooks
129/139	Violence

135 Lennie said quietly: 'It ain't no lie.'
Lennie is quite articulate about the prospect of living 'on the fatta the lan'', although he is actually repeating often-heard words. Are you surprised by Lennie's ability to express himself in this way? These words now assume a new significance, given the reality of George's farm, and the idea begins to attract Crooks too and he invites Lennie to sit down. The fact that Lennie is disobeying George's instruction to keep the farm a secret gives this episode an increased sense of tension.

134/136	Crooks
133/145	Dreams
132/136	Lennie

136 Crooks settled himself more comfortably . . .
Crooks is by nature proud and reserved. He is lonely and decides that he can tell Lennie secrets by way of conversation that will not then be revealed or

135/137	Crooks
135/138	Lennie

turned against him in ridicule. Crooks is yet another character whose life is isolated and unsatisfying, like that of Candy.

104/138	Loneliness

137 Crooks leaned forward over the edge . . .

This account provides us with background information about Crooks. He is not typically a black rooted in slavery, but has enjoyed a higher standard of living and status. Blacks are rare in California and in this area of Soledad, he explains. Even so, the family were victims of prejudice and this was reinforced by the disapproval of his father for his white friends. Colour prejudice undermines Crooks's position.

130/140	Aspects of style
136/138	Crooks

138 Crooks laughed again.

Crooks is correct in his assessment of Lennie; he has not understood the revelations about Crook's background. Lennie is in a state of innocence, and the injustices of the world are not part of his perceptive consciousness. Crooks continues to lower his guard and shows us through his talk to Lennie that he suffers intense loneliness. He suggests that Lennie and George are partners for the 'unspoken' companionship of being with one another. He sees his own black skin and physical deformity as a double disadvantage.

137/139	Crooks
130/141	George
136/141	Lennie
136/142	Loneliness

139 His voice grew soft and persuasive.

Crooks cannot resist the novel opportunity to inflict pain on another; he is usually the victim but his suggestion to Lennie is nevertheless vindictive and heartless.

138/140	Crooks
134/141	Violence

140 Crooks bored in on him. 'Want me ta tell ya . . .'

Such a prediction is portentous – Crooks unwittingly predicts how Lennie will be treated. But Lennie will not just be tied up like a dog, but shot in the manner of Candy's dog.

137/141	Aspects of style
139/142	Crooks
133/143	The natural world

141 Suddenly Lennie's eyes centred and grew quiet . . .

Without the presence of George, Lennie is unprotected from this attack. Crooks is playing a dangerous trick on him in an attempt to see how steadfast the relationship is between Lennie and George. Lennie is deeply moved by this maliciously presented hypothesis and is stirred to menacing action in defence of his friend. The incident demonstrates to us that in certain circumstances Lennie's anger can be roused and he is then prepared to act. From this incident we can get a better understanding of George's responsibility, and the hopelessness of Lennie's condition.

140/156	Aspects of style
138/154	George
138/143	Lennie
139/159	Violence

142 Crooks saw the danger as it approached him.

This certainly is a cry from the heart from Crooks and he is very explicit about the pain of loneliness.

140/144	Crooks
138/144	Loneliness

143 Lennie growled back to his seat . . .

The familiar animal/bear imagery is again applied to Lennie. Is there a hint of circus performance in his return to the barrel like a dangerous animal? Notice the parallel – when George first got to know Lennie he used to 'have a hell of a lot of fun with 'im' too – not unlike the way Crooks does here.

141/145	Lennie
140/149	The natural world

	Characters and ideas previous/next comment	

144 Crooks said gently: 'Maybe you can see now.'
Here is a further disclosure from Crooks about the particular isolation of his position at the ranch. He craves for companionship. He shows us that conversation is a necessary part of being human – it acts as a confirmation of what each individual perceives and believes. Without such a possibility of reference to other people 'he got nothing to measure by'.

142/145   Crooks
142/146   Loneliness

145 The stable buck went on dreamily: . . .
Crooks has, in his youth, enjoyed the environment, experience and companionship that George, Lennie and Candy hope to achieve. Notice how Lennie is able to pick out certain things from George's frequent speculations.

144/146   Crooks
135/146   Dreams
143/148   Lennie

146 'You're nuts.' Crooks was scornful.
In some ways Crooks has put his enforced isolation to good use and what he says here contains insights into realism, psychology and philosophy. He makes comparisons between hope and religion and relates the quest for 'a little piece of land' to the quest for heaven. He has a fairly cynical view of each aspiration. However, his experience and observations do create tension and apprehension in the plot, because George, Lennie and Candy seem to be so near to realizing their dreams.

145/147   Crooks
145/153   Dreams
144/149   Loneliness

147 'Ya mean the big guy?'
Crooks is disappointed that his companionship, newly gained, is threatened by intrusion.

146/149   Crooks

148 Candy stood in the doorway . . .
The difference between Candy and Lennie in their approach to the harness room is interesting. Candy is aware of the distance between himself and the black while Lennie has an innocent disregard for it.

133/149   Candy
145/150   Lennie

149 'Come on in.'
The division between the two men consciously remains, but Crooks is excited by the possibilites brought about by the unaffected behaviour of Lennie. In the light of Crooks's loneliness, the grimness of which he has just related to Lennie, this statement is heavily ironic. The room represents an enforced isolation that Crooks does not enjoy. On the other hand Candy has just gone through the traumatic experience of losing his dog and privacy for him would have been very welcome.

148/150   Candy
147/151   Crooks
146/156   Loneliness
143/155   The natural world

150 Lennie broke in: 'You said . . .'
With Candy the age-old prejudices have prevented any communication. It takes the action of Lennie to bring the two men together. Part of Lennie's function, then, is to act as a catalyst to the relationship of others.

149/162   Candy
148/160   Lennie

151 Crooks said darkly: . . .
This response is to be expected. Crooks is cynical about the disregard of the others on the ranch.

149/153   Crooks

152 Candy quickly changed the subject.
This further contributes to Slim's depth of character and our sense of his

120/163   Authority

fairness. It sets him apart from the other men, and, linked to the action of the boss, gives him a natural authority.

120/206	Slim

153 Crooks interrupted brutally.
Crooks returns to the theme of aspiration and the remote possibility of such a dream becoming reality.

151/157	Crooks
146/155	Dreams

154 'Yeah?' said Crooks. 'An' where's George now?'
Despite the fact that George has a desperate need to accumulate money quickly, he has gone 'out on the town'. He has said, though, that he intends only to sit and drink. Crooks's reflection upon the poverty of the itinerant workers would appear to contain a considerable amount of truth.

141/175	George

155 Candy cried: 'Sure they all want it.'
This idea is a central theme of the book. The ownership of land, and the opportunity to see the seasons through, would give status and self-esteem to the low-paid workers. It would promote enthusiasm and pride in their work, and the farming process would provide incentive and fulfilment.

153/156	Dreams
149/160	The natural world

156 Crooks asked: 'You say you got . . .'
The probability of successfully moving to the 'dream farm' seems remote for Lennie, George, and Candy. Few have achieved it before – none in Crooks's experience – yet they do seem so near, with only one month's further savings necessary. This contributes to the sense of tragedy in the book.

As in most of Steinbeck's novels, the main image of the book is a kind of earthly paradise which, for Americans, usually meant a network of small farms, worked by their owners for their own benefit. It is a vision of prosperity and harmony which embraces good fellowship and the independence of the individual. But in Steinbeck's novels, as Crooks puts it: 'Nobody never gets to heaven.' (See comment 101 for further explanation on this sentence.)

141/167	Aspects of style
155/157	Dreams
149/157	Loneliness

157 Crooks reached around and explored his spine . . .
Despite his experience and cynicism, Crooks is drawn in to the same dream of a better life and companionship. In the course of this episode, he has moved from sullen resentment to companionable excitement. His isolation and rejection which we see at the beginning of the novel are a façade to conceal the frustrations of loneliness.

153/168	Crooks
153/163	Dreams
156/170	Loneliness

158 'Any you boys seen Curley?'
The description of her face and breathing accentuate the sensuous passion of Curley's wife. Abandoned on the ranch, she, too, is lonely and looking for company.

122/159	Curley's wife
157/159	Loneliness

159 She stood still in the doorway . . .
Curley has abandoned her for a visit to old Susy's place. Does he prefer the company of prostitutes to her? No wonder she is vicious in the way she attacks those others who have been left behind. Is she, like them, some sort of 'weak one'? Is it a challenge to them to act 'strongly'? Curley's arrogance and unfeeling neglect is characteristic, and indicates that there is a very poor

120/162	Curley
158/161	Curley's wife
158/161	Loneliness
141/161	Violence

basis for his marriage. She is not looking for her husband, she is looking for male company – this could be to satisfy her passionate nature, or to strike back at Curley, who has left her behind. Which do you think it is, or do you sense that she is herself unsure?

---

160 Lennie watched her fascinated; . . .
Lennie responds to her overt sexuality whenever she appears. She is particularly provocative. This, given Lennie's disposition, is a potentially dangerous state of affairs.

150/165	Lennie
155/162	The natural world

---

161 Lennie watched her fascinated; . . .
She adopts another provocative pose with 'hands on hips'. This extract says as much about her as it does about the men. She is dangerous, and knowing her can result in being beaten up by her husband. What she claims, though, about them being 'scared of each other' seems to point to another aspect of their loneliness – it seems to suggest that the men make a conscious choice to remain solitary. The casual nature of their work and their restless drifting means that none are able to build up trust easily.

159/162	Curley's wife
159/162	Loneliness
159/170	Violence

---

162 The girl flared up.
This reinforces the psychology of Curley's disposition. His size means that he constantly feels the need to prove himself. Physique is very important to him. He is obsessed by establishing his supremacy (like an animal) and, presumably, his 'ownership' of his wife is another facet of this. She is obviously desirable and accentuates this by her dress and manner. She is yet another character who is craving companionship but her sex, and Curley, are complications and frustrations in her search for friendship, as she has indicated. She seems to need to captivate men and behaves alluringly, as if to reassure herself about her impact. (This is *not* a sexist view: the evidence is present in the way she behaves each time she appears.)

150/164	Candy
159/183	Curley
161/163	Curley's wife
149/174	Loneliness
160/171	The natural world

---

163 'Awright,' she said contemptuously.
Curley's wife parallels the ranch-hands in her loneliness and the dream of a better life that she describes. She must be of limited intelligence – even in 1930 'offers of film parts' was a cliché. She is abusive, showing her need to establish her supremacy. To what extent do you feel that she and her husband Curley are two of a kind?

152/169	Authority
162/165	Curley's wife
157/164	Dreams
162/170	Loneliness

---

164 Lennie watched her, his mouth half open.
Candy derives comfort, strength and self-respect from the prospect of farm ownership. His reaction demonstrates well the needs of the ranch-hand.

162/166	Candy
163/171	Dreams

---

165 Lennie watched her, his mouth half open.
Throughout this episode Lennie remains transfixed by the appearance of Curley's wife.

163/166	Curley's wife
160/167	Lennie

---

166 Curley's wife laughed at him.
The hopelessness of the ranch-hand and the poverty of his life is expressed by several different characters. Curley's wife takes comfort and satisfaction from deriding Candy's hope.

164/174	Candy
165/167	Curley's wife

167 Lennie looked up guiltily. 'Who – me?'
This exchange has rooted in it the events which will lead to the story's tragic climax. Curley's wife's hard look has the effect of causing Lennie 'embarrassment'. The communication has sexual undertones, particularly in view of her intention to talk to him later. She is attracted by someone who can defeat Curley. Why do you suppose this is?

168 Lennie smiled happily.
Having selected her target in Lennie, Curley's wife begins to make suggestive comments. Lennie would not understand the significance of the allusion, but obviously Crooks does.

169 Crooks stood up from his bunk . . .
Perhaps Crooks has derived some strength from his exchanges with Lennie and Candy. Certainly he is now exerting a pressure which hitherto has been uncharacteristic. But by attempting to control Curley's wife, a white woman, he is putting himself at great risk. Notice how his move has been prompted by a wish to defend Lennie.

170 She turned to him in scorn.
The great personal advances that Crooks has made in the last few pages, encouraged by the open nature of Lennie and the friendship of Candy, are taken away by what Curley's wife says. She re-establishes the oppressive domination of white over black. It is typical of Curley's wife that her power stems from sexual manipulation and innuendo. Her threat of 'framing' Crooks, alleging sexual interference, would be sufficient to get him lynched. We are prepared by this for the getting together of the lawless lynching mob that pursues Lennie at the end of the novel; just like the lynching mob in Weed, they will be intent on killing him.

171 Candy subsided. 'No,' he agreed.
Lennie, who throughout this section has exhibited sometimes surprising conversational skills and a growing sense of confidence, as Candy and Crooks involve him in their shared dream, is reduced to the state of a helpless child. Notice how Steinbeck uses the word 'whined' to contribute to the animal imagery which appears in the descriptions of Lennie throughout the book.

172 Candy stepped over to him.
Curley's wife conducts herself with appalling venom throughout this episode and her behaviour has the effect of negating the growing confidence of the men planning to move out to George's farm. In wielding this devastating control and belittling first Crooks, then Candy and Lennie in this fashion, she is paving the way for the ultimate destruction of Lennie at the end of the book.

173 She turned to Lennie.
Curley's wife gives further encouragement to Lennie by congratulating him on the injury that he inflicted on her husband. This all contributes to the growing sense of tension, and we can only look upon such intimacy with apprehension. The horses, in their unrest, seem to sense the unnaturalness of her behaviour, and react to her dangerous presence.

174 'The gate banged,' Candy said, . . .
The transformation we have witnessed, in the move from reluctance to readiness to share his ideas with Lennie and Candy, illustrates how Crook's personality has been deadened and suppressed by years of antagonism and oppression. The emancipation that Crooks has experienced through the idea of the 'dream farm' has now left him, and the old prejudices make him withdraw into himself. The magical interlude, and hope for the future, has been destroyed by the bigoted nature of Curley's wife. Curley's wife is renowned for her lack of moral scruples – she pursues the ranch-hands and there are some suggestions that she was perhaps like this before her marriage to Curley. Candy attempts to relieve the tension she has created by his innuendo and the comment '. . . Curley's wife can move quiet. I guess she had a lot of practice . . .'.

175 In a second George stood framed . . .
In reprimanding Candy, George unconsciously supports Curley's wife's prejudice. He, of course, does not want anyone to know because he feels that they may be sacked as a consequence if the boss hears of their plans to quit as soon as they have enough money. Crooks misinterprets what is meant, conditioned as he is to expect nothing but harsh rejection from the whites.

176 The three men went out of the door.
Crooks's rejection of the whites and his withdrawal into his former state is completed with this exchange. He returns to his application of the liniment. This activity brackets, or encapsulates, the recent events. Stillness and peace are re-established at the end of the scene.

Section 5

This section opens in the great barn, where Lennie has just petted his puppy to death. Curley's wife unburdens herself to Lennie, rather like Crooks did. This results in her death and the start of the man-hunt for Lennie.

Commentary

177 It was Sunday afternoon.
This section, too, starts with scene-setting that is rich in description. Notice how Steinbeck appeals to our sense of hearing as well as sight. The visual detail emphasizes the size of the barn and this is supported by the onomatopoeia of 'nibble', 'wisp', 'stamped', 'bit', 'rattled', 'buzz' and 'humming'. (Onomatopoeia is the making up of words which sound like the action or idea being described.) It all adds up to create a warm and friendly pastoral environment.

178 Only Lennie was in the barn, . . .
The action of the men, who appear as intruders in the pastoral calm (just like in section one) is underlined by the contrasting sounds of 'clang', 'shouts' and 'jeering'. The barn is a fitting environment for the gentle and uncomplicated nature of Lennie. Notice that Steinbeck has carefully placed Lennie in this quiet, idyllic setting, sitting 'under a manger'. Is there any significance in Steinbeck's particular choice of this place, do you think?

179 And Lennie said softly . . .
Lennie has killed the puppy by petting it. His ability to inflict death through love is escalating.

180 He unburied the puppy . . .
This is a moment of great pathos. Lennie's need to express love has killed the puppy, and he knows that the consequences, when George finds out, could be severe. He is struggling to come to terms with the enormity of his action – particularly his disobedience. The unrest that the event has caused prepares Lennie, psychologically, for the next scene with Curley's wife. Curley's wife is attracted to Lennie because of the injury he inflicted on her husband. She knows the habits of the men (she *does* spend a long time watching them) and has worked out a complex strategy for her safe entanglement with Lennie in the barn. But Lennie sees the consequences of disobedience and tries to comply with George's instructions. Curley's wife is lonely, and her action of kneeling beside him in the hay is very provocative.

181 Curley's wife came round the end . . .
Steinbeck has prepared Lennie for this meeting. He has prepared us too, by creating a 'tragic' atmosphere filled with unease because of Lennie's instability. Appropriately, Curley's wife wears her 'bright cotton dress' and 'red ostrich feathers'. We know that Lennie is attracted to the colour red. Her face is 'made-up', and her 'curls' are in place. She has made herself as seductive as possible.

182 She said quietly: 'He's scared . . .'
Curley's wife is like an animal seeking out the physical leader of the pack.

183 'I get lonely,' said she.
The loneliness of Curley's wife is brought about by the actions of her husband. She is treated as his possession, and is prevented from talking to others because of his jealousy. Perhaps the lack of trust is caused by absence of love as well as her general behaviour.

184 Then all of Lennie's woe came back on him.
Lennie is particularly vulnerable because of his state of mind. He is sad because of the death of the puppy and also because of the possible exclusion from the joy of the 'dream farm'. This makes him receptive to the offer of company and comfort.

185 'He was so little,' said Lennie.
Notice how this episode describing the death of the puppy is a parallel of what is going to happen to Curley's wife. Steinbeck uses this incident not only to show us more about the character of Curley's wife, by letting us see her vulnerable side and her humanity in consoling Lennie, but also as a way of giving the scene tension and a potential for danger.

186 Her face grew angry.
Curley has kept his wife under very strict control. When she gets the opportunity to converse the words pour out in a 'passion of communication'. In what almost amounts to a soliloquy from a play (Lennie really isn't paying any attention to most of what she says) Curley's wife reveals her own dreams of a better life. Notice how they are a parallel to those expressed by George, Candy and Crooks. Notice also how Steinbeck has used this technique of an 'almost-soliloquy' before; can you remember with whom? (Think of the people who share the dream.) Curly's wife has been star-struck, and she appears to have taken seriously the various promises made by men ingratiating themselves with her. Although she derides the dreams of the men, deep inside, she is no different from them. She likes to act a part. Do you think George was really right about her being 'jail bait'?

Of Mice and Men is a deceptively simple work. It is more than just a straight-forward tale of the simple-minded Lennie and his loyal friend George. Many Californian place-names have their origins in the languages of Spain and Mexico. Soledad, where the action of the book takes place, means 'Our Lady of Loneliness'. The name refers to the mother of Christ, especially during that part of her life between Good Friday and the Resurrection (Easter Sunday). Bearing this in mind, do you think that there is any significance in the fact that *Of Mice and Men* begins late on a Friday afternoon and ends on the following Sunday?

187 She went on with her story quickly, . . .
Curley met his wife at a dance hall, the evening that she decided not to stay at home any longer. She has not the wit (or wish?) to realize that the men had made empty promises, and that they had sent no letters. Curley's offer was convenient for escape. However, she 'don' *like* Curley'. As with Crooks, Lennie's innocent and open manner invites the confidence of Curley's wife. Which other character has a manner which invites people to confide in him? Are there any similarities between Lennie and this other character, do you think?

Characters and ideas	
previous/next comment	
162/187	Curley
182/184	Curley's wife
180/186	Loneliness
183/186	Curley's wife
175/186	Dreams
180/187	Lennie
181/186	Aspects of style
182/194	The natural world
185/187	Aspects of style
184/187	Curley's wife
184/188	Dreams
183/0	Loneliness
186/189	Aspects of style
183/192	Curley
186/188	Curley's wife
184/189	Lennie

188 'Well, I ain't told this to nobody before.'
Curley's wife has derived her 'dream' from the glittery world of show-business, the cinema and glossy magazines. Notice how it contrasts sharply with the idea of the farm which preoccupies the three men. Her interest in the world of the cinema and acting perhaps gives us a clue to her behaviour – which appears to be designed, like her clothes, to provoke interest rather than to invoke intimacy. Despite her sensual movements she only wants to 'talk'.

187/190	Curley's wife
186/189	Dreams

189 She asked: 'What makes you so nuts about rabbits?'
Lennie again describes how he likes to 'pet' things. He has moved from mice through the puppy and now dreams only of owning rabbits. The fact that those which attracted him at the fair had 'long-hair' is a skilful touch by Steinbeck – it helps with the transition of Lennie's desire from rabbits to people via the long hair of Curley's wife.

187/193	Aspects of style
188/193	Dreams
187/190	Lennie

190 Curley's wife moved away from him a little.
Previously she has snuggled up to Lennie, but now she begins to become alarmed at the absorption with petting that he shows. Curley's wife does not appear to see the danger in Lennie's preoccupation and her own closeness to him. She does not appreciate that Lennie's obsession with 'petting' will extend to her! She describes him as a big baby, but this underestimates the interest and fascination with which he has observed her in the past.

188/191	Curley's wife
189/191	Lennie

191 Curley's wife laughed at him.
This is a difficult moment to understand. How unconscious is her suggestion that Lennie might fondle her hair? Is she innocently referring to its texture, or is she deliberately leading Lennie on to a sexual encounter? The question is crucial, yet unanswerable, and points to an ambivalence in her character. Is she in the barn just to talk to Lennie, or is she intent upon seduction?

190/192	Curley's wife
190/192	Lennie

192 Lennie's big fingers fell to . . .
In stroking the hair of Curley's wife, Lennie reminds us of how Curley kept his left hand soft for such an action himself, and how Lennie usurped him, having crushed that hand. Petting is at the centre of Curley's marriage, but is uncontrollable in Lennie. Curley's wife only struggles when her appearance is 'mussed up', which fits in with her general demeanour and her dreams. Is everything about Curley's wife superficial?

187/208	Curley
191/197	Curley's wife
191/193	Lennie

193 Lennie was in a panic.
We have been prepared for this inevitable climax by all the evidence about Lennie's character in the novel. His panic results in an explosion of strength and the result, as with the puppy, is fatal. As anger takes over so his strength increases. It is important for us to notice that the reason for his panic and anger is the thought of the possibility that George may discover that Lennie has broken his promise to him. George uses the 'dream farm' and its rabbits to control Lennie's actions; do you think this use of psychology has been inappropriate? Ironically, it is just this kind of concern which leads to the death of Curley's wife. In an effort to stop her screaming, Lennie uses more and more strength until, finally, her neck is broken.

189/199	Aspects of style
189/194	Dreams
180/194	George
192/194	Lennie

194 He looked down at her, . . .
Lennie knows the difference between right and wrong and realizes the enormity of his action. He is also aware that his action will enrage George,

193/199	Dreams
193/200	George

who will punish him. Notice how Steinbeck uses 'pawed' to remind us of the animal imagery which always surrounds Lennie and his actions.

195 From outside the barn . . .

It is typical of Lennie that whilst knowing 'good' and 'bad' he is unable to discriminate between degrees of severity. Ludicrously, he leaves in order to conceal the body of the puppy thinking that the evidence of its death will make his position worse. There is no difference for him between animal and human life. Notice how this has the effect of making the death of Curley's wife sadder, because of the way Lennie regards it.

196 The sun-streaks were high on the wall by now, . . .

This descriptive passage of the tranquillity of nature and animals contrasts with the harshness of the drama that has just taken place. Visually, the scene is dusk and the sounds are more distant and in harmony. The dog responds to the scent of death by protecting its vulnerable young. Notice how the way the bitch moves reminds us of the way Lennie tends to behave in his animal state of innocence.

197 Curley's wife lay with a half-covering . . .

Curley's wife is also restored to her natural state of innocence by death. She had been forced away from this natural state of grace by her predicament and her ambitions. Her death does not result in a horrific sight, rather it is described in an idyllic setting, and the physical description of her body emphasizes this.

198 As happens sometimes, a moment settled . . .

Notice how Steinbeck's writing technique is very similar to script-writing for the cinema. We have seen how he carefully constructs settings for each main section of the book and only then introduces characters. Here he is trying to achieve a punctuation of the action by introducing what in a film would be a 'freeze-frame'. This has the effect of creating a pause before we move on to the turbulence of the story's conclusion.

199 From around the end of the last stall . . .

As the action is restarted, it is ironic that Candy should be working out more details about the feasibility of the farm – which would, of course, have been Lennie's salvation. All their hopes are dashed by the discovery of the body. Look at how Steinbeck uses a gathering sense of sound to accompany the restarting of the action: the noises get louder, from 'stamped' and 'chinked' to 'stamped and snorted', 'chewed' and 'clashed'.

200 George said: 'What was it . . .'

Look carefully at how Steinbeck removed George temporarily from the novel (for about thirty pages) in order to give Lennie the opportunity for autonomous (that is self-directed) action. Now George returns and confesses that what has happened was a possibility and a worry that had been in the back of his mind. George shows the depth of his concern for Lennie and hopes that he will now be imprisoned and cared for. Do you feel that this course of action would be wrong for Lennie? He has, after all, been linked to the unspoilt wildness of nature throughout the novel. Or would Lennie never have been safe, even on the 'dream farm'? What would your reaction

Characters and ideas	
previous/next comment	
193/195	Lennie
185/195	The natural world
194/196	Lennie
194/196	The natural world
193/198	Aspects of style
195/200	Lennie
195/197	The natural world
192/199	Curley's wife
196/200	The natural world
196/199	Aspects of style
198/213	Aspects of style
174/201	Candy
197/205	Curley's wife
194/202	Dreams
194/203	George
196/204	Lennie
197/202	The natural world

have been if you had been George? What would you have hoped would happen to Lennie next?

---

201 But Candy said excitedly: . . .
Candy is a realist. Whilst George believes that there may be some way of putting Lennie into care, Candy knows that the ranch-hands, led by Curley, will exact their own brutal kind of justice. Lennie will be shot and/or lynched.

| 199/205 | Candy |
| 180/207 | Violence |

---

202 Now Candy spoke his greatest fear.
The book is full of the sympathetic and sometimes dream-like portrayal of nature and the men's hope for their idyllic farm. Candy, and at one time Crooks, both suggest that these things are the book's central symbols. Certainly the idea of a 'heaven' (Crooks's word) has motivated the men and given them hope. Because of Curley's wife, Lennie has sinned. Lennie's action robs the men of their promised escape. Their place was going to be a heaven where black and white and the sick of mind and the sick of body would all be restored to full humanity, where all would be made whole and equal.

| 199/205 | Dreams |
| 200/210 | The natural world |

---

203 George didn't answer his question.
At this moment George realizes that his true prospects are no better than all the other itinerant workers, with their limited aspirations of cheap sex and gambling. Notice how George is quick witted enough to devise a strategy that will protect him from any suggestion of blame. Is he being callous here do you think, or realistic?

| 200/209 | George |

---

204 Candy said: 'He's such a nice fella.'
Lennie is a 'nice fella'. The circumstances of the book and the idiosyncrasies of Lennie's character have brought about the dreadful conclusion. George asserts that Lennie was never motivated by ill-intent; the victims are casualties of his innocence. Without getting weighed down in over-complicated interpretations, can you come to any conclusion about whether the innocent are always victims of their own innocence? In any situation in life where one person, or a group of people, are 'innocent' (in the sense that Steinbeck has depicted it) is it always their very innocence which is their greatest liability? Is Steinbeck's view of life therefore essentially cynical and bitter or can you find hope for the future anywhere in this story? What might happen to George after all this?

| 200/208 | Lennie |

---

205 Old Candy watched him go.
Candy's bitter attack on Curley's wife hints at her symbolic role in the novel. Through her action of 'messing things up', he and his friends have lost the dream and therefore the possibility of escape. Is Curley's wife unfairly condemned here, do you think?

201/213	Candy
199/206	Curley's wife
202/217	Dreams

---

206 Then Slim went quietly over to her, . . .
Slim, the only ranch-hand with natural authority, investigates and confirms, by his actions, the death of Curley's wife. All respect his knowledge as the leader of the group. Even allowing for the emotional involvement of Curley, notice the contrast between the basis of Slim's authority and that of

170/207	Authority
205/0	Curley's wife
152/211	Slim

Curley – Slim's way is quiet and firm, but Curley's way is always the way of immediate violence.

---

207 Curley came suddenly to life.
The possibility of a hunt and the opportunity to use his Luger seems to have animated Carlson. Carlson seems to solve all problems with his gun. His keenness to use the Luger on Candy's dog is parallelled here by his enthusiasm to use it on Lennie. Notice how Carlson's immediate reaction was to run and get his gun.

206/219	Authority
109/220	Carlson
201/208	Violence

---

208 Curley came suddenly to life.
Curley's response is aggressive: he already has a score to settle with Lennie. Rather than letting the law take its course, Curley announces his intention of shooting Lennie in the stomach with a shot-gun. This would lead to a very brutal, painful and cruelly extended death.

Notice how much like a thirties' film-script Curley's dialogue is during this scene, with phrases like 'All right, you guys, . . .'.

192/210	Curley
204/209	Lennie
207/210	Violence

---

209 Slim turned quietly to George.
George agrees with Slim that Lennie's actions are in keeping with tendencies already displayed, particularly in Weed. But George has a further plan in mind, because he sends the men in the opposite direction to Lennie's hide-out. See if you can decide whether George's difficulty in speaking is caused by the fact that he runs a great personal risk by lying, or by his own uncertainty about whether or not he is acting for the best.

203/212	George
208/211	Lennie

---

210 Slim nodded. 'We might,' he said.
Curley treats this hunt as an animal hunt – but he is out to inflict a dreadful injury on Lennie as a punishment before he dies.

208/212	Curley
202/211	The natural world
208/212	Violence

---

211 Slim nodded. 'We might,' he said.
Slim is perceptive. He knows that to take Lennie alive and to lock him up would not really be the answer. Slim can see that it would be wrong to 'cage' Lennie – he talks of the capture as if it were of an animal. He appears to be suggesting that the most humane treatment would be to kill him.

209/214	Lennie
206/221	Slim
210/214	The natural world

---

212 'I know,' said George. 'I know.'
Curley's resolve to 'shoot for his guts' by way of revenge, dispels any hope for George that Lennie is going to survive the man-hunt. Curley's instruction to George puts him in the correct place for the final element of the drama.

210/0	Curley
209/213	George
210/213	Violence

---

213 Whit said excitedly: 'I ain't got a gun.'
George does all he can to gain assurances from the men that they will take Lennie alive and do him no harm. Candy was in a similar position when asking for a reprieve for his old dog. No one would take his side either.

199/214	Aspects of style
205/0	Candy
212/216	George

Section 6

*The final section returns to the setting at
the start of the book. In a way which
echoes the shooting of Candy's dog,
Lennie has been 'taken outside' into the
world of nature, where he belongs, and shot.*

Commentary

214 The deep green pool of the Salinas River . . .
This description sets the scene for the final action of the novel and the death of Lennie. It is worth comparing this description with that at the start of the book. The pastoral calm is still evident, but the action of the heron swallowing the little water-snake hints at the violence in nature. The silence of the original setting is disturbed by the 'gust' of the wind, and the noise of the leaves, as found at the end of the pastoral scene described at the beginning of the book.

The suggestion is that all life returns to this pool. Notice how suggestive is the effect of the paragraph which begins 'A far rush of wind sounded . . .'. To see what is meant, imagine the effect this activity would have if it were part of a scene in a film. By ending the novel at the place where it began, Steinbeck suggests that the action of the book has come full circle. This gives a feeling of completeness to the story, but does it also give us this feeling about the lives of the characters? Think about whether the effect of the book is to suggest that they are forever doomed to wander from farm to farm, through season after season, casual acquaintance after casual acquaintance, endlessly repeating the hopeless cycle of their lives without ever getting anywhere.

215 Suddenly Lennie appeared out of the brush, . . .
Lennie's movements are described once more in the terms of 'a creeping bear'. His action in drinking is superbly contrasted to that at the book's opening. This time, instead of throwing himself into the water, he drinks as a real wild animal might–cautiously, and listening to every sound. His movements are those of a bear, including his posture, which allows him to see the entrance to the watering area. His mind returns to the events of the opening of the novel, with its conflict between ideas about 'crime' and 'ketchup'. Notice how the animals in the clearing abandon him.

216 And then from out of Lennie's head . . .
Steinbeck once again uses a film technique to illustrate the complex nature of Lennie's mentality. The guilt of his actions and their consequences is played out in a scene between Aunt Clara (his former guardian) and himself. Aunt Clara takes on the character and words of George–although, interestingly, not his voice. Perhaps Lennie has heard this scene over and over again from George. Notice how the first vision is concerned with events in the past. Lennie's conscience (if that is what it is) explains in detail how he has sinned.

Why is this curious dream-like state injected into this final action? Does it appear to you as an original and effective piece of writing by Steinbeck, or do you regard it as out of place–too bizarre and therefore confusing? Whichever way you view it, it is important that you think through your ideas. You should, for example, be able to explain *why* you feel the way you do about Steinbeck's use of this device. Does Lennie's dream or vision add anything to what we know or feel about him? Think about whether it has the effect of making Lennie appear more innocent, child-like, and vulnerable. Would the story's end have been sadder or more positive if this episode had been omitted, do you think?

217 Aunt Clara was gone, and from out of . . .
Lennie's second vision articulates his fear for events in the future. The rabbit is a symbol of an era of peace in a serene and natural habitat – both past and future. (Why 'past'? Hint: think about the kinds of toy which children have.) Lennie tells himself that this dream has been shattered because of what he has done. He appears to be achieving some kind of analytical grasp of reality, although he is forced to think in pictures. This development could be the result of his traumatic experiences. Notice how both Aunt Clara and the rabbits also featured prominently in the early pages of the book.

205/219	Dreams
216/218	Lennie
215/220	The natural world

218 Only the topmost ridges were . . .
This is almost identical to a section near the start of the book, except that now the distant sounds of men are not inconsequential, but indicate the pursuit by the hunting-party. George, to reassure Lennie, moves through familiar exchanges to a point where they talk once again about how they have each other for support and companionship. Notice how Steinbeck manages to convey George's anguish at what is happening – with light touches here and there, using words and phrases like 'he said woodenly', 'quiet for a moment', 'shakily'. Notice also how, for once, George speaks to Lennie calmly and quietly, without his usual outbursts, calling him by name instead of by the more usual 'crazy bastard' and 'son-of-a-bitch', which George uses when angry. Is George often this gentle with Lennie? On what sorts of occasion does he treat him with such consideration?

216/219	Aspects of style
216/219	George
217/219	Lennie
212/222	Violence

219 The little evening breeze blew . . .
As the hunting-party gets nearer, the 'dream farm' takes on the attributes of Heaven, and becomes a haven where Lennie will attain peace. George has stolen Carlson's Luger and has therefore prepared himself for this final act of friendship. He asks Lennie to remove his hat to expose the back of his head and the area pointed out by Carlson on Candy's dog. In dreaming of the future Lennie is at his happiest and his least suspecting.

Notice how Steinbeck mirrors not only the act of shooting Candy's dog and Lennie, but also draws skilful parallels with the emotions which motivate the various killings in the book. George kills Lennie, Lennie has killed Curley's wife, and Slim has passed judgment on (and directed) both killings. All three are involved in killing out of a kind of affection, understanding, love or compassion – in other words they are innocent of evil motives.

218/0	Aspects of style
207/0	Authority
217/0	Dreams
218/220	George
218/220	Lennie

220 'Go on, George. When we gonna do it?
As predicted by Carlson, a shot at the back and base of the skull administers a humane death – one without 'quivering'. The rewards for Lennie in such an action are that there will be '. . . no more trouble. Nobody gonna hurt nobody, nor steal from 'em', as he puts it. These things would, of course, have been their rewards from their occupation of the 'dream farm'. Notice the heavy irony of Lennie's urgings to George to 'do it now'.

This final scene, as previously discussed, was foreshadowed by the one in which Candy's dog was shot. Notice how Candy admitted to George that 'I ought to of shot that dog myself, George. I shouldn't ought to of let no stranger shoot my dog.' This may be part of the reason why George shoots Lennie, but what might the other part be? (Think about what Curley threatened.) George seems torn between genuine affection for Lennie (and his promise to Aunt Clara to care for him) and a desire to be free of a troublesome and inconvenient burden. When he shoots Lennie, he has made a choice between two dreams; the dream of the farm has, by force of circumstance, been rejected and the other one about lonely independence, about endless games of solitaire has been dully accepted: 'I'll set in some pool-room till ever'body goes home.'

207/222	Carlson
219/221	George
219/0	Lennie
217/0	The natural world

The world in which *Of Mice and Men* is set is one in which characters do not exist in the same state of innocence and purity which we see described in the natural world. The itinerant workers seem condemned to wander forever in search of their greatest desire – their heaven, their home. Theirs seems to be a world at times full of senseless violence in which, eventually, death comes to mice and men alike.

221 'I just done it,' George said tiredly.

George has the strength of character and the quick wit to present a plausible explanation for Lennie's death. Slim sees the significance of the placing of the shot and sees through the proffered explanation. His perception, and his caring and reassurance, sustain George as they leave the rest of the party.

220/0   George
211/0   Slim

222 Curley and Carlson looked after them.

Carlson's final observations express the nature of the lives which he and Curley live – filled as they are with barbarism, callousness and brutality. They are unable to understand the world of George and Slim, because they cannot see the basis upon which it is built. Curley and Carlson are all the more poignantly lonely because of their ignorance of their own loneliness.

220/0   Carlson
218/0   Violence

Characters in the novel

This is a very brief overview of each character. You should use it as a starting point for your own studies of characterization. For each of the aspects of character mentioned you should look in your text for evidence to support or contradict the views expressed here, and indeed, your own views as well.

Know the incidents and conversations which will support and enlarge upon your knowledge of each character. You will find it helpful to select a character and follow the commentary, referring always to the text to read and digest the context of the comment.

Candy

Candy is near to the end of his useful life on the farm and has few prospects. The loss of his hand stresses the casual violence of the ranch-workers' lives. He has little to look forward to; at the beginning of the ranch episode in the novel he loses his dog and thus the only companionship he has enjoyed. He is given renewed comfort, strength and self-respect by the prospect of his part-ownership of the farm with Lennie and George. Just as he realistically appraises his own prospects for the future early in the novel, he later predicts a particularly grim end for Lennie at the hands of the mob.

Carlson

Carlson is used by Steinbeck to illustrate, in a very economical way, the callous barbarity of the lives of the ranchers. He is an outspoken trouble-maker who aggravates tension in the knowledge that he has sufficient ability to defend himself adequately. He is both practical and unsentimental, and he takes a pride in his gun and his ability to inflict death upon the old and innocent. The possibility of a man-hunt at the end of the novel appears to excite and animate him.

Crooks

Crooks is a literate, black cripple who tends horses on the ranch. He has long been the victim of oppressive violence and prejudice and has retired behind a stern façade which is both aloof and reserved, his essential personality having been deadened and suppressed by years of antagonism. He has known better times, and unlike most Southern blacks, was brought up on a smallholding run by his father. The nature of his past home is similar to that sought after by Lennie, George and Candy and, despite his initial cynicism, Crooks too becomes caught up in this dream of escape. It is soon apparent in the novel that his initial rejection of friendship or company when it is proffered is more to do with the anguish and frustration of loneliness than anything else. Once encouraged, he reveals that he possesses a good understanding of his life and the life of a ranch-hand generally, observations which he has formulated and considered at length during long hours of solitude. He is articulate and evidently has a well-disciplined intellect. His new-found confidence and self-respect lead him to attempt to control the intrusion of Curley's wife, but this is thwarted by her vicious threats, and his recently won optimism is finally defeated by George's dismissive attitude towards the suggestion that he might also participate in running their 'dream farm'.

Curley

Curley is small of stature and appears to have developed an inferiority complex as a result. He is constantly aggressive, and constantly looking for an opportunity to assert what he sees as his masculinity. Humiliated by his wife's apparent dissatisfaction and unhappiness, Curley needs to boost his self-esteem and confidence. His stance is that of a professional fighter – he was once a boxer – but significantly when he is using this skill he fights unfairly, taking advantage of the meek whilst carefully avoiding the strong. He seems vindictively dedicated to inflicting the maximum amount of damage and pain possible, to, dispel the frustration and anger he feels for his own situation. He attempts to maintain authority through violence and even his approach to intimacy is crude and physical – as evidenced by his glove which, according to Candy, is full of vaseline.

Curley's wife

Curley's wife is not named throughout the novel, and this reinforces our view of her as Curley's possession. She is not treated as an individual in her own right, which is something she bitterly resents, but is seen (perhaps even by the author) as a symbol of other things – a temptress, a chattel, a sex-object, or a piece of 'jail bait'. Most of her actions are involved in some way in a betrayal of her marital status. She flaunts herself around the ranch in inappropriate attire, flirting with the ranch-hands and conscious of its effect. Her whole demeanour is sensual and she exerts influence by sexual manipulation and innuendo. There is, however, evidence in her meeting with Lennie in the barn to suggest that she does not have a real desire to seduce but instead just wants attention. Her major preoccupation is in devising strategies which are designed to avoid her detection by her husband so as to allow for assignations with the ranch-hands should that be their wish; and she executes this ploy by the masterful device of always seeming to be looking for him!

She reveals, too, that she has dreams of a better, more fulfilling existence, but in her case these dreams are provided by glossy film magazines and the easy promises of men she has known in the past. Her ambition to work in films or the music-hall derives from her desire to be admired. This wish to be the centre of attention is partly rooted in vanity and partly in insecurity and loneliness, brought about by her husband's inadequacies and censorious behaviour. We do not know, apart from the ranch-hands' speculations, how far she would pursue her assignations with the men, given the chance. Our only opportunity to find out, at her meeting with Lennie in the barn, is described with very skilful ambiguity by Steinbeck. Certainly her general posture and conduct is full of sensual promise, and although her panic at Lennie's petting of her hair leads to her downfall, this could have been caused by Lennie's unconscious roughness rather than by any decision on her part that events had gone too far.

George

George is quick-witted and intelligent. His stance suggests vigilance and nervous caution and gives the impression that this is in part derived from his endurance of physical hardship in the past. He has a good working knowledge of the environment and his love of the stillness and harmony of the pastoral scene gives weight to his dream to own and work a small farm, supervising the crops from planting through the natural cycle to harvesting. He appears to know how to cope with such a life, and wants to exchange the monotony of his present existence for it. He is very aware of the low expectations and aimless life-style which is typical of the itinerant farm-worker.

He has taken on the responsibility for Lennie partly out of pity and partly for companionship, and he has the strength of mind and character to carry through his strategy of the compassionate killing in the final chapter, utilizing his knowledge of Carlson's expertise and his weapon.

George can be seen as an incomplete person, like Lennie. Indeed, it is possible to see that in many ways they are the two incomplete halves of one whole, contented person. If you imagine a fusing of their two personalities and physical attributes then it becomes clear that where one is strong the other is weak. In the opening sequence of the book we can also see that they are similar in appearance too, and in the way they move – Lennie is in many ways George's 'shadow'. George represents the head or intelligence of the two, whilst Lennie's nature is intensely physical – he is the body. This understanding of their natures shows us the error of assuming that George is exploiting Lennie, as the boss suspects, and we are prevented from seeing their relationship as sentimental because of the intensely practical sense of realism which

George has. George knows that Lennie is both a hinderance and an advantage to him and his feelings for Lennie never become sentimental or mawkish.

It must be admitted, though, that George is not entirely blameless for the disastrous end which befalls Lennie. He is aware of the strong tendencies which Lennie has to behave in certain ways, and senses upon their arrival at the ranch that the ingredients that could add up to immense trouble are present. He chooses to ignore the signs – his need for a 'stake' is greater than the influence of his natural caution. For one night he even abandons the vulnerable Lennie, despite his full knowledge of the circumstances which exist at the ranch, and which lead to his downfall.

Lennie

Although to some extent Lennie's behaviour is child-like, he does demonstrate some aspects of adult maturity, and this ultimately results in his death. Despite his terror of violence he is a man of great physical strength – the strength, Steinbeck suggests, of a bear. He is frequently described in animal terms and this would indicate not only his bear-like capacity for holding on to his prey and inflicting great damage, but also a kind of bear-like innocence coupled with a total unconcern for any sort of morality, which means that the ordinary values of 'good' and 'bad' are difficult to attribute to him. His dominating obsession for 'petting' indicates deep, emotional needs, which Lennie himself may not understand but which, nevertheless, have to be satisfied. There is a dreadful progression in the novel from dead mouse to dead girl, and there is little doubt that the sexuality of Curley's wife and her desire for attention contribute heavily to the tragic climax of the novel. It is 'tragic' because Lennie's downfall can be charted by his fatal desire to 'pet': this is the overwhelming flaw in his personality which collides with the flawed ambitions of Curley's wife to be petted and admired.

At the opening of the novel Lennie is characterized by naïvety and innocence; by the end he has fallen from grace (he has committed murder) and by this act has deprived himself of the paradise of the 'dream farm'. There is no way he can escape retribution. An interesting question to consider here is how far do we feel that Lennie is ever really innocent? Certainly he seems often to be ignorant of the consequences of his actions and never seems able to learn from the unfortunate incidents in which he becomes involved. He never learns, for example, that his 'petting' of creatures always leads to their death. Do you feel that Lennie is innocent or mentally retarded? Is it possible for him to be both simultaneously?

Slim

Slim is majestic and charismatic, and exerts his natural authority through a gentleness and friendliness that contrasts with the fundamental and pervasive violence which shapes the lives of the other characters. As a master craftsman amongst the other workers, he has a natural dignity that demands respect. In times of conflict or stress it is to Slim that the ranch-hands turn, and his magnanimous tolerance of their shortcomings is demonstrated by the easy care he exhibits for all those who need his attention and support. He is a man of great perception and has an intuitive sense of justice and fairness. He is a central moral force in the novel.

The boss

The boss appears once only in the book, unless you assume that Curley, as his son, is his representative in a more immature form. Certainly the boss and Curley seem to share the same aggressive and intolerant nature and their dress has similarities in the high-heeled boots which, interestingly, the boss is said to wear 'to prove he was not a labouring man'. What is interesting is the use of the word 'prove', as this is what Curley seems to spend much of his time trying to do – prove himself.

Whit

Whit is little more than a foil. His conversations are used by Steinbeck as a dramatic device to provide passages of exposition (or description). His character is never developed and he acts rather as the boss does, but in an even more minor way; his is a cameo role – he is a 'character' who represents a certain type in the world of the ranch-hands.

What happens
in each section

Steinbeck wrote *Of Mice and Men* in a form which was an experiment in what he referred to as the 'play-novelette' form, that is, it is a play which is written in the physical pattern of a novel. This means that the novel is organized as a series of different scenes or acts, with each one having some 'stage directions' to explain the 'setting of the scene', with characters having 'entrances' and 'exits' just like on a stage. *Of Mice and Men* has in fact been produced as a play, with very little change needing to be made to the original pages of the book. There are many interesting devices which remind us of the theatre in addition to the entrances, exits and scene-setting mentioned. For example, we have a kind of soliloquy (Curley's wife exposes her inner soul but Lennie doesn't listen), a form of Chorus (George has to recount past events to Lennie, who has forgotten), and we find many pieces of description which sound exactly like 'direction' to a camera.

Some editions of the book have split the text into chapters, which equate with the sections below, whilst some run the text together into one long piece of prose. As the sections all begin with a piece of description, rather akin to the cinematic 'establishing shot' at the start of a new location, you will have little problem in finding your way around the book whichever format your edition adopts.

Section 1　Through detailed description, rich in natural imagery, this section establishes the pastoral nature of the environment and generates a sense of harmony. Lennie and George are introduced and the complementary nature of their characters is indicated. Lennie has recently been in trouble and both men are on the run from the township of Weed, where they had their last employment. They have been tricked by a bus driver who dropped them several miles from their destination – a ranch where they have permits for work. George, obviously of superior intelligence and experience, is caring for Lennie, a slow-witted giant of a man, and both men look forward to a time when they will have their own small farm – at this moment this seems more like a dream than an actual possibility. Their aspirations appear in the form of a recital which is told in the style of a ritual bed-time story between parent and child. Some parts of the description of this promised world are contributed by Lennie who has learned them by heart. The two men spend the night sleeping under the stars.

Section 2　Lennie and George arrive at the bunk-house, and meet the old-timer Candy who reveals that the boss is angry at their late arrival. They install their belongings and the boss arrives to interview them. George has prearranged with Lennie that he alone will take on the responsibility of answering the boss's questions, but this tactic backfires and only excites the boss's curiosity about Lennie, who eventually speaks, much to George's annoyance. Curley, who is the boss's son, is introduced into the novel, and his initial exchanges with the two men soon become acrimonious. On his departure George and Lennie learn that Curley has recently married and, Candy informs them, his wife is already giving him trouble and causing general anxiety around the ranch by her behaviour. Curley's conduct and situation alerts George to potential danger, and he tells Lennie to keep well out of harm's way and especially to keep away from Curley. Curley's wife makes a brief appearance to look the new men over but leaves hurriedly because her husband seems to be looking for her. George, concerned about her manner, warns Lennie about tangling with her also. Although by now the circumstances at the ranch are obviously hostile, their need for work and money outweighs George's inclination towards leaving. Slim enters the action of the novel and his nobility and kindness to some extent bring calmness to the atmosphere. The fact that Slim's dog has had puppies prompts another ranch-hand, Carlson, to suggest that they should offer one to Candy as a replacement for his dog, an aged sheepdog which is past its useful life, and which the men believe should be put down. The action concludes with a further confrontation between Curley and George.

Section 3　This scene is set in the bunk-house, and it is evening. Slim has given Lennie a puppy and this act of kindness prompts George to confide in him about Lennie's background and the recent trouble he has caused. Slim, with his quiet, assured manner invites such confidences. Lennie enters, concealing the newly acquired puppy, but he is made to return it to its mother, as it is too young to survive away from her.

Carlson enters and puts forward his argument for destroying Candy's dog, and suggests exchanging it for a new puppy. He disregards Candy's alarm and hurt feelings and eventually, after demonstrating the humane way in which he would dispatch the dog by shooting it in the back of the head, takes the dog outside. Conversation dies away, and there is an uneasy silence amongst the circle of men. Further attempts at conversation falter and the tension increases as the men wait for the sound of a gunshot. Little noises dominate the silence, and then a distant shot is heard. With the execution of the dog there is an easing of the tension and George and another hand, Whit, play cards and discuss the character of Curley's wife. George is endeavouring to discover details of their situation in an attempt to ascertain the amount of danger to Lennie. Whit describes the alternative arrangements that exist for securing female company and gives George details of 'Susy's place', a saloon where men can sit and drink, or pay for other favours from the five girls employed there.

There follows an extended period of calm in the bunk-house, punctuated by the brief appearance of Curley who is, as usual, looking for his wife, whom he suspects of having some secret assignation – on this occasion with Slim. Meanwhile Slim is actually out in the barn tending an injury to a horse's hoof. George, sensing trouble, warns Lennie again about tangling with Curley. Their conversation turns to the hoped-for farm that one day they will work and own. The presence of Candy, silent and grief-stricken at the loss of his dog, has been forgotten by George and a sudden question from him makes both men jump. George, nervous about making their private ambitions public, eventually responds to Candy's questions, and reveals that he has a specific and available small farm in mind. The dream becomes a real possibility as Candy explains that he has a sum of money saved and that he would be happy to invest it in exchange for a place at the farm. George slowly realizes that his long-hoped-for dream is now an actual possibility. They agree to keep their intentions secret from their employers.

The happiness of the men is shattered by the reappearance of Curley, who is still searching for his wife. Curley has been humiliated by Slim and is unable to challenge the threats of Carlson; he turns in a cowardly way on Lennie and fights him viciously. Lennie is badly hurt but does not defend himself until he hears George's desperate command. He reaches out and restrains any further assault from Curley by grasping his hand. In his panic he will not release the hand until George's shout finally breaks through to him. Slim is horrified at Lennie's innate strength and takes care of Curley. To avoid further trouble and embarrassment, Slim concocts a story that Curley's injury was caused by an accident with a piece of machinery.

Section 4   After the turmoil of the last section this scene opens peacefully, and is set in the harness room of the barn, which is Crook's room. There are only the sounds of the horses, for the men have gone to 'Susy's place' leaving the 'damaged' characters (Crooks, Candy and Lennie) behind. Curley's wife has also been abandoned. Being a solitary man Crooks at first does not welcome company but eventually he lowers his defences and allows Lennie and then Candy to join him. They talk, first about Lennie's and George's partnership and, with the appearance of Candy, about the proposed purchase of the farm. Crooks cynically rejects the possibility that they will succeed in their venture, but he too becomes involved to a point where he offers his services free in exchange for a part in their plan. This reverie is interrupted by the sudden appearance of Curley's wife, aggrieved by the departure of her husband, who has gone to town with the other hands. She takes a delight in abusing the men but when she is rebuked by them complains of her unhappiness and loneliness caused by her marriage to Curley. She is anxious to find out the truth about her husband's hand – probably with the idea that here, at last, is someone to control him and with whom she might enjoy some sort of diversion. Frustrated in her quest, she returns to abuse and when Candy, in a rage provoked by her jibes, tells of their plans, she adopts the same cynical pose as that taken up initially by Crooks. The bruises on Lennie's face give Curley's wife the answer she is looking for with regard to who damaged her husband's hand, and she makes clear her interest in Lennie. Crooks, with new-found self-esteem and confidence, becomes hostile towards her because of this but she instantly humiliates and emasculates him by suggesting that, by lying about his behaviour, she could easily get him lynched. The men are made to feel aware of their vulnerability once again and are beaten by her attack. She leaves, but has destroyed the new-found friendliness and confidence of the men. George arrives, looking for Lennie, and his annoyance caused by the open discussion of his once-secret plans is sufficient to make Crooks return to his self-pitying meditation and his application of liniment in isolation from the others.

Section 5   The penultimate section opens in the setting of the great barn. Outside the men are engaged in a game of throwing horseshoes, but inside Lennie sits in some distress. He has killed the puppy recently given to him, by too much petting, and is distraught. Curley's wife appears, carefully dressed for maximum impact and appeal. Lennie is reluctant to converse with her because of his promise to George, but she convinces him that they are safe from Curley and that, anyway, Lennie could very easily inflict further injury on him if he became difficult. She wants to talk and she tells Lennie bitterly of the opportunities for a glamorous life that have passed her by; she reveals that she does not even like Curley. Lennie's single-minded adherence to the prospect of having rabbits that may be immune to his petting eventually riles her; her 'true confessions' have had no impact. She tries a fresh approach, humouring Lennie's preoccupations with petting and touching and offers him her own hair. However, she becomes alarmed when Lennie disturbs it by stroking it excessively, and in crying out for him to stop she panics him. He holds on firmly and in the struggle to keep her quiet his uncontrollable strength breaks her neck. Remembering George's instructions about hiding if there is trouble, he creeps from the barn and returns to the clearing described at the start of the book.

The body of the girl is discovered by Candy whilst he is looking for Lennie, and before he raises the general alarm he alerts George. In the death of Curley's wife, George sees all his hopes shattered. He arranges for Candy to tell the rest of the men about the incident, and thereby gives himself time to get away from the scene of the crime, thus avoiding suspicion. The men enter the barn in a group, with George following in the rear. Slim examines the body and the men form a posse to hunt down Lennie. Curley is enraged by the death of his wife and proposes to blast Lennie in the stomach with his shotgun. This would cause Lennie an agonizing and slow death, which is Curley's intention, although the general excuse for shooting to kill is that they believe he is armed with Carlson's gun, which is discovered to be missing. The men, reluctantly accompanied by George, leave for the man-hunt.

Section 6   For the final action of the story we return to the setting of the opening scene in the book. Lennie appears and, after cautiously drinking, squats down where he can see the entrance to the clearing. He is tormented first by an imagined vision of Aunt Clara, who consigned him to the care of George, and then by the vision of a large rabbit which chastizes him for his actions. George approaches and reassures Lennie about their comradeship and says he is not cross. The men talk once more of their dreams and when Lennie is looking out over the water, mentally lost in the future, George shoots him in the back of the head in the style of the execution of Candy's dog at the hands of Carlson. The men, whose noisy approach has intruded throughout this scene, believe George's account of how he disarmed Lennie and killed him. Only Slim is perceptive enough to be aware of the enormity of the truth, and he takes George away to comfort him. Curley and Carlson, immune to violence and brutality, wonder at the other men's distress.

Coursework and preparing for the examination

If you wish to gain a certificate in English literature then there is no substitute for studying the text/s on which you are to be examined. If you cannot be bothered to do that, then neither this guide nor any other will be of use to you.

Here we give advice on studying the text, writing a good essay, producing coursework, and sitting the examination. However, if you meet problems you should ask your teacher for help.

Studying the text

No, not just read–study. You must read your text at least twice. Do not dismiss it if you find a first reading difficult or uninteresting. Approach the text with an open mind and you will often find a second reading more enjoyable. When you become a more experienced reader enjoyment usually follows from a close study of the text, when you begin to appreciate both what the author is saying and the skill with which it is said.

Having read the text, you must now study it. We restrict our remarks here to novels and plays, though much of what is said can also be applied to poetry.

1 You will know in full detail all the major incidents in your text, **why**, **where** and **when** they happen, **who** is involved, **what** leads up to them and what follows.

2 You must show that you have an **understanding of the story**, the **characters**, and the **main ideas** which the author is exploring.

3 In a play you must know what happens in each act, and more specifically the organization of the scene structure–how one follows from and builds upon another. Dialogue in both plays and novels is crucial. You must have a detailed knowledge of the major dialogues and soliloquies and the part they play in the development of plot, and the development and drawing of character.

4 When you write about a novel you will not normally be expected to quote or to refer to specific lines but references to incidents and characters must be given, and they must be accurate and specific.

5 In writing about a play you will be expected both to paraphrase dialogue and quote specific lines, always provided, of course, that they are actually contributing something to your essay!

To gain full marks in coursework and/or in an examination you will also be expected to show your own reaction to, and appreciation of, the text studied. The teacher or examiner always welcomes those essays which demonstrate the student's own thoughtful response to the text. Indeed, questions often specify such a requirement, so do participate in those classroom discussions, the debates, class dramatizations of all or selected parts of your text, and the many other activities which enable a class to share and grow in their understanding and feeling for literature.

Making notes

A half-hearted reading of your text, or watching the 'film of the book' will not give you the necessary knowledge to meet the above demands.

As you study the text jot down sequences of events; quotations of note; which events precede and follow the part you are studying; the characters involved; what the part being studied contributes to the plot and your understanding of character and ideas.

Write single words, phrases and short sentences which can be quickly reviewed and which will help you to gain a clear picture of the incident being studied. Make your notes neat and orderly, with headings to indicate chapter, scene, page, incident, character, etc, so that you can quickly find the relevant notes or part of the text when revising.

Writing the essay

Good essays are like good books, in miniature; they are thought about, planned, logically structured, paragraphed, have a clearly defined pattern and development of thought, and are presented clearly – and with neat writing! All of this will be to no avail if the tools you use, i.e. words, and the skill with which you put them together to form your sentences and paragraphs are severely limited.

How good is your general and literary vocabulary? Do you understand and can you make appropriate use of such terms as 'soliloquy', 'character', 'plot', 'mood', 'dramatically effective', 'comedy', 'allusion', 'humour', 'imagery', 'irony', 'paradox', 'anti-climax', 'tragedy'? These are all words which examiners have commented on as being misunderstood by students.

Do you understand 'metaphor', 'simile', 'alliteration'? Can you say what their effect is on you, the reader, and how they enable the author to express himself more effectively than by the use of a different literary device? If you cannot, you are employing your time ineffectively by using them.

You are writing an English literature essay and your writing should be literate and appropriate. Slang, colloquialisms and careless use of words are not tolerated in such essays.

Essays for coursework

The exact number of essays you will have to produce and their length will vary; it depends upon the requirements of the examination board whose course you are following, and whether you will be judged solely on coursework or on a mixture of coursework and examination.

As a guide, however your course is structured, you will be required to provide a folder containing at least ten essays, and from that folder approximately five will be selected for moderation purposes. Of those essays, one will normally have been done in class-time under conditions similar to those of an examination. The essays must cover the complete range of course requirements and be the unaided work of the student. One board specifies that these pieces of continuous writing should be a minimum of 400 words long, and another, a minimum of 500 words long. Ensure that you know what is required for your course, and do not aim for the minimum amount – write a full essay then prune it down if necessary.

Do take care over the presentation of your final folder of coursework. There are many devices on the market which will enable you to bind your work neatly, and in such a way that you can easily insert new pieces. Include a 'Contents' page and a front and back cover to keep your work clean. Ring binders are unsuitable items to hand in for **final** assessment purposes as they are much too bulky.

What sort of coursework essays will you be set? All boards lay down criteria similar to the following for the range of student response to literature that the coursework must cover.

Work must demonstrate that the student:

1 shows an understanding not only of surface meaning but also of a deeper awareness of themes and attitudes;

2 recognizes and appreciates ways in which authors use language;

3 recognizes and appreciates ways in which writers achieve their effects, particularly in how the work is structured and in its characterization;

4 can write imaginatively in exploring and developing ideas so as to communicate a sensitive and informed personal response to what is read.

Much of what is said in the section **Writing essays in an examination** (below) is relevant here, but for coursework essays you have the advantage of plenty of time to prepare your work – so take advantage of it.

There is no substitute for arguing, discussing and talking about a question on a particular text or theme. Your teacher should give you plenty of opportunity for this in the classroom. Listening to what others say about a subject often opens up for you new ways to look at and respond to it. The same can be said for reading about a topic. Be careful not to copy down slavishly what others say and write. Jot down notes then go away and think about what you have heard, read and written. Make more notes of your own and then start to clarify your own thoughts, feelings and emotions on the subject about which you are writing. Most students make the mistake of doing their coursework essays in a rush – you have time so use it.

Take a great deal of care in planning your work. From all your notes, write a rough draft and then start the task of really perfecting it.

1 Look at your arrangement of paragraphs, is there a logical development of thought or argument? Do the paragraphs need rearranging in order? Does the first or last sentence of any paragraph need redrafting in order to provide a sensible link with the preceding or next paragraph?

2 Look at the pattern of sentences within each paragraph. Are your thoughts and ideas clearly developed and expressed? Have you used any quotations, paraphrases, or references to incidents to support your opinions and ideas? Are those references relevant and apt, or just 'padding'?

3 Look at the words you have used. Try to avoid repeating words in close proximity one to another. Are the words you have used to comment on the text being studied the most appropriate and effective, or just the first ones you thought of?

4 Check your spelling and punctuation.

5 Now write a final draft, the quality of which should reflect the above considerations.

Writing essays in an examination
Read the question. Identify the key words and phrases. Write them down, and as they are dealt with in your essay plan, tick them off.

Plan your essay. Spend about five minutes jotting down ideas; organize your thoughts and ideas into a logical and developing order – a structure is essential to the production of a good essay. Remember, brief, essential notes only!

Write your essay
How long should it be? There is no magic length. What you must do is answer the question set, fully and sensitively in the time allowed. You will probably have about forty minutes to answer an essay question, and within that time you should produce an essay between roughly 350 and 500 words in length. Very short answers will not do justice to the question, very long answers will probably contain much irrelevant information and waste time that should be spent on the next answer.

How much quotation? Use only that which is apt and contributes to the clarity and quality of your answer. No examiner will be impressed by 'padding'.

What will the examiners be looking for in an essay?
1 An answer to the question set, and not a prepared answer to another, albeit slightly similar question done in class.

2 A well-planned, logically structured and paragraphed essay with a beginning, middle and end.

3 Accurate references to plot, character, theme, as required by the question.

4 Appropriate, brief, and if needed, frequent quotation and references to support and demonstrate the comments that you are making in your essay.

5 Evidence that reading the text has prompted in you a personal response to it, as well as some judgment and appreciation of its literary merit.

How do you prepare to do this?

1 During your course you should write between three to five essays on each text.

2 Make good use of class discussion etc, as mentioned in a previous paragraph on page 75.

3 Try to see a live performance of a play. It may help to see a film of a play or book, though be aware that directors sometimes leave out episodes, change their order, or worse, add episodes that are not in the original – so be very careful. In the end, there is no substitute for **reading and studying** the text!

Try the following exercises without referring to any notes or text.

1 Pick a character from your text.

2 Make a list of his/her qualities – both positive and negative ones, or aspects that you cannot quite define. Jot down single words to describe each quality. If you do not know the word you want, use a thesaurus, but use it in conjunction with a dictionary and make sure you are fully aware of the meaning of each word you use.

3 Write a short sentence which identifies one or more places in the text where you think each quality is demonstrated.

4 Jot down any brief quotation, paraphrase of conversation or outline of an incident which shows that quality.

5 Organize the list. Identify groupings which contrast the positive and negative aspects of character.

6 Write a description of that character which makes full use of the material you have just prepared.

7 What do you think of the character you have just described? How has he/she reacted to and coped with the pressures of the other characters, incidents, and the setting of the story? Has he/she changed in any way? In no more than 100 words, including 'evidence' taken from the text, write a balanced assessment of the character, and draw some conclusions.

You should be able to do the above without notes, and without the text, unless you are to take an examination which allows the use of plain texts. In plain text examinations you are allowed to take in a copy of your text. It must be without notes, either your own or the publisher's. The intention is to enable you to consult a text in the examination so as to confirm memory of detail, thus enabling a candidate to quote and refer more accurately in order to illustrate his/her views that more effectively. Examiners will expect a high standard of accurate reference, quotation and comment in a plain text examination.

Sitting the examination

You will have typically between two and five essays to write and you will have roughly 40 minutes, on average, to write each essay.

On each book you have studied, you should have a choice of doing at least one out of two or three essay titles set.

1   **Before sitting the exam**, make sure you are completely clear in your mind that you know exactly how many questions you must answer, which sections of the paper you must tackle, and how many questions you may, or must, attempt on any one book or in any one section of the paper. If you are not sure, ask your teacher.

2   **Always read the instructions** given at the top of your examination paper. They are

there to help you. Take your time, and try to relax – panicking will not help.

3 **Be very clear about timing, and organizing your time.**

(a) Know how long the examination is.
(b) Know how many questions you must do.
(c) Divide (b) into (a) to work out how long you may spend on each question. (Bear in mind that some questions may attract more marks, and should therefore take proportionately more time.)
(d) Keep an eye on the time, and do not spend more than you have allowed for any one question.
(e) If you have spare time at the end you can come back to a question and do more work on it.
(f) Do not be afraid to jot down notes as an aid to memory, but do cross them out carefully after use – a single line will do!

4 **Do not rush the decision** as to which question you are going to answer on a particular text.

(a) Study each question carefully.
(b) Be absolutely sure what each one is asking for.
(c) Make your decision as to which you will answer.

5 **Having decided which question** you will attempt:

(a) jot down the key points of the actual question – use single words or short phrases;
(b) think about how you are going to arrange your answer. Five minutes here, with some notes jotted down will pay dividends later;
(c) write your essay, and keep an eye on the time!

6 **Adopt the same approach** for all questions. Do write answers for the maximum number of questions you are told to attempt. One left out will lose its proportion of the total marks. Remember also, you will never be awarded extra marks, over and above those already allocated, if you write an extra long essay on a particular question.

7 **Do not waste time** on the following:

(a) an extra question – you will get no marks for it;
(b) worrying about how much anyone else is writing, they can't help you!
(c) relaxing at the end with time to spare – you do not have any. Work up to the very moment the invigilator tells you to stop writing. Check and recheck your work, including spelling and punctuation. Every single mark you gain helps, and that last mark might tip the balance between success and failure – the line has to be drawn somewhere.

8 **Help the examiner.**

(a) Do not use red or green pen or pencil on your paper. Examiners usually annotate your script in red and green, and if you use the same colours it will cause unnecessary confusion.
(b) Leave some space between each answer or section of an answer. This could also help you if you remember something you wish to add to your answer when you are checking it.
(c) Number your answers as instructed. If it is question 3 you are doing, do not label it 'C'.
(d) Write neatly. It will help you to communicate effectively with the examiner who is trying to read your script.

Glossary of literary terms

Mere knowledge of the words in this list or other specialist words used when studying literature is not sufficient. You must know when to use a particular term, and be able to describe what it contributes to that part of the work which is being discussed.

For example, merely to label something as being a metaphor does not help an examiner or teacher to assess your response to the work being studied. You must go on to analyse what the literary device contributes to the work. Why did the author use a metaphor at all? Why not some other literary device? What extra sense of feeling or meaning does the metaphor convey to the reader? How effective is it in supporting the author's intention? What was the author's intention, as far as you can judge, in using that metaphor?

Whenever you use a particular literary term you must do so with a purpose and that purpose usually involves an explanation and expansion upon its use. Occasionally you will simply use a literary term 'in passing', as, for example, when you refer to the 'narrator' of a story as opposed to the 'author' – they are not always the same! So please be sure that you understand both the meaning and purpose of each literary term you employ.

This list includes only those words which we feel will assist in helping you to understand the major concepts in play and novel construction. It makes no attempt to be comprehensive. These are the concepts which examiners frequently comment upon as being inadequately grasped by many students. Your teacher will no doubt expand upon this list and introduce you to other literary devices and words within the context of the particular work/s you are studying – the most useful place to experience and explore them and their uses.

Plot   This is the plan or story of a play or novel. Just as a body has a skeleton to hold it together, so the plot forms the 'bare bones' of the work of literature in play or novel form. It is however, much more than this. It is arranged in time, so one of the things which encourages us to continue reading is to see what happens next. It deals with causality, that is how one event or incident causes another. It has a sequence, so that in general, we move from the beginning through to the end.

Structure   The arrangement and interrelationship of parts in a play or novel are obviously bound up with the plot. An examination of how the author has structured his work will lead us to consider the function of, say, the 43 letters which are such an important part of *Pride and Prejudice*. We would consider the arrangement of the time-sequence in *Wuthering Heights* with its 'flashbacks' and their association with the different narrators of the story. In a play we would look at the scene divisions and how different events are placed in a relationship so as to produce a particular effect; where soliloquies occur so as to inform the audience of a character's innermost emotions and feelings. Do be aware that great works of fiction are not just simply thrown together by their authors. We study a work in detail, admiring its parts and the intricacies of its structure. The reason for a work's greatness has to do with the genius of its author and the care of its construction. Ultimately, though, we do well to remember that it is the work as a whole that we have to judge, not just the parts which make up that whole.